SPHERE COLOUR
GROWING F

C000003876

SPHERE BOOKS LIMITED
30-32 Gray's Inn Road, London WCIX 8JL

Contents

Introduction

Quite simply this book is designed to save you considerable investment in plants and to increase your enjoyment of gardening.

More and more people are turning to growing from seed not just because of the savings in hard cash that they can make but also because of the pride they can gain from seeing the whole process through from beginning to end.

Buying a plant from a nursery or garden centre can be very convenient. It can also save you a lot of time. But it means you will never be able to look on that plant as your own. Someone else sowed the seed, nurtured and developed it.

Buying a plant from a nursery is also enormously restricting. Few garden centres — however large — will be able to carry a fraction of the varieties in plant form that stand in serried rows of seed packets on their shelves.

It means you will have to select from a very limited range.

If you haven't tried growing from seed you may be amazed at how easy the whole process is, as long as you observe some simple basic rules. But when you think about it, why shouldn't it be simple? The process happens quite simply and naturally in the wild without any fuss. Reproducing that process in your own home, greenhouse or seed-bed, with the aid of modern knowledge and equipment, only makes the process easier — and more enjoyable.

This book will tell you all you need to know about growing from seed. We explain how to prepare your plot, how to sow — both indoors and outdoors — how to look after your seedlings so you get the healthiest plants, and we explain about weed control and pests and diseases.

We also give you a month-by-month guide to sowing and harvesting.

We give advice on equipment and talk about the use of fertilisers and composts. And we also tell you something of the history of seeds going back to the times BC when man first started to grow from seed. The main feature of this book, however, is a comprehensive guide to 120 flowers and vegetables which boasts full colour pictures of each and detailed, easy-to-use advice on everything you need to know to get the best results. Each flower and vegetable has a potted biography which explains how to grow, what conditions they like, when to sow and when to transplant, what growing care they need and when to harvest. It's an invaluable guide to growing from seed which you will want to consult again and again.

HISTORY

It is generally agreed that agriculture in it broadest sense first started about nine thousand years ago in a fertile belt stretching from what is now Iraq up to Turkey. Soon after India, China and Egypt and then Peru and Mexico caught on. Sadly, we Europeans took rather longer to learn. In due course the early growers developed simple tools — a digging stick, rudimentary hoes and the early plough. Initially the cultivation was restricted to root products like the yam and simple pulses and fruits. These were easy to grow in the warm, humid climates and required only the most basic implements. Gradually more sophisticated tools and techniques were developed and the interaction between different cultures, as travel and communications spread out around the world, meant that ideas and plants were exchanged. At one time most seeds would have been scattered or broadcast, ironically a method now finding favour once again, but slowly new devices and methods were introduced culminating in machines with wheels which not only made the drill but which planted the seeds as well. Early growers may just have scattered seeds and hoped for the best blaming a fickle god if there was a bad harvest. But we know that, certainly as early as 2,000 BC, fairly sophisticated knowledge existed about the needs and the treatment of seeds. We know, for instance, that the Greek Theophrastus recommended to his friends the idea of soaking cucumber seeds in milk or water to speed up germination.

In early times almost anything that did not prove poisonous was probably eaten but it meant some very bitter meals. Gradually the idea of developing and improving that which was found pleasant, instead of suffering that which wasn't, grew. Early agriculture, however, was very much devoted to satisfying the stomach and it wasn't until later that the idea of growing to please the eye found much favour.

Nowadays seeds can be bought in a number of pre-treated forms ie pre-positioned on strips of paper to make sowing more reliable. It may be a modern idea but there is nothing new about it. The Roman writer Columella gave an account in the first century BC of how to form thorny, quickset hedges out of brambles, wild roses and Christ thorn. The seeds were to be mixed with a powder made by grinding up vetch seeds. This was then mixed with water and smeared onto old rope and left to dry. The rope was then stored. Where the hedge was to be grown furrows were dug and left fallow over winter. In early spring the dried ropes were placed along the bottom of the furrows and then covered with soil. It's a remarkable account which shows a sophisticated understanding of seedsmanship. Columella also gave detailed advice on transplanting seedlings which is as relevant today as it was over 2,000 years ago. Cabbages and lettuces, for instance, were to be transplanted when they had developed six leaves.

The names might be the same but it's certain that the cabbages and lettuces we know now are very different. Cabbages, for instance, are thought to have developed almost exclusively from the wild Brassica oleracea, a perennial shrub with bitter tasting leaves found near the coast of the Mediterranean and Atlantic. Before it became palatable this bitter shrub must have undergone considerable development. In the 4th century BC Theophrastus records that only two types of cabbage existed. By AD 70 Pliny was writing about lots of different types. Even in that relatively short time many new cabbages had been developed. The same story can be told about most of the plants and vegetables we know now. Pulses, for instance, are among the very earliest vegetables to have been cultivated.

Records date them on archaeological sites as early as 7,000 BC, in the case of lentils, and 5,000 BC in the case of kidney beans.

Official records show that the oldest viable seeds came from Southern Manchuria. Three lotus seeds believed to be 466 years old were successfully germinated in 1982. Claims have been made for much older seeds including germination of "mummy" wheat seeds from the Pyramids but these have never been scientifically tested.

Many vegetables are developed from families which we nowadays would regard as garden flowers. For instance, the lily family gave birth to onions, leeks, garlic, chives and asparagus and the vast daisy family is responsible for the lettuce. Nor is this process over. The development of flowers and vegetables continues apace.

SOWING

Raising plants from seed is not only the cheapest way of stocking your garden it is also the most satisfying. For most people the process will begin in the depths of winter browsing through the seed catalogues, planning what to grow and designing a cropping plan.

Growing from seed is also a very simple, straightforward process as long as you follow some basic rules. A seed needs air, warmth and moisture in order to germinate successfully.

Once it has emerged it will then need light in order to make healthy sturdy growth. Beyond this, seeds will vary significantly in their needs, the time they should be sown and the treatment they should be given. They also differ in the way in which they should be sown. Very fine seeds need to be scattered and lightly firmed in, while seeds with hard coats like sweet peas will germinate quicker if the skin is nicked with a penknife. Some can be sown in pots, some indoors, some outdoors. For full details see our individual listings on pages 19–78.

A wide range of plants can be grown from seed. Garden plants can be grouped into three main categories: annuals, biennials and perennials. Annuals are those which will complete their full life-cycle from sowing to seeding within a year. Biennials will complete their life cycle within two years but always more than one.

Virtually all real annuals and biennials can be raised from seed. Perennials are those which grow for more than two years and while many perennials can be grown perfectly well from seed like bedding dahlias and bedding begonias, many more should be reproduced vegetatively. The commonest method of vegetative reproduction is taking cuttings. Named varieties like border dahlias cannot properly be reproduced from seed.

Seeds fall into a number of categories. Most seed bought from the shop comes in packets. Always buy from a reputable dealer. ''Bargain'' packets may well have had a lengthy shelf life. Some seeds will have been dusted with a fungicide, or fungicide and insecticide combination, and this will be called 'dressed' seed. Other seeds can be bought in pellet form.

They have been coated with a clay mixture to allow for easier sowing. This is especially common with the smaller seeds. Pellet seed should remove the need for thinning. Seed can be saved — there is usually some left after sowing — but make sure that you put it in an airtight container and keep it in a cool, dry place. Some seed can be collected from your plants. Collect from annuals and perennials when the seeds are ripe, dry thoroughly and store in a cool dry place in an airtight container. Never save seeds of F1, F2 or other hybrids.

They are unlikely to grow the same as the parent plant.

Sowing Outdoors

When buying, select seeds which will best suit your soil and local weather conditions. Consult the packet details and your supplier. The temptation to experiment with new and relatively untried varieties can bring disaster so keep to well-tried onces for bulk sowing. Restrict experiments to just a few plants. In some cases you may be sowing into a seed bed, in others

direct into the growing site. Seed beds are essentially a way of saving space though some plants specifically need this treatment. The seed bed will need to be carefully prepared in fertile soil which is free of clods and stones and well raked. To ensure good root development add a dressing of 3 oz. superphosphate per square yard and rake well in. Cover with a mulch to preserve the tilth if not planting immediately. The size of your seed bed needs to suit the size of your plot if it is to be efficient and not either waste space or fail to supply your needs. A bed measuring 5 ft. x 5 ft. can take nine rows of 30 plants. Space the rows 6 ins. apart. Cover with netting to protect.

When sowing direct into your plot the most common method used will be in straight drills made with a trowel or hoe. The seeds are simply dropped into the bottom of the drill. Depth varies according to size of seed and we give full details in our individual listings. Best results will always be obtained in moist warm soil. When wet and cloggy, seeds are likely to be attacked by pests and diseases while if too dry they simply won't germinate. Adding peat or sowing compost can help to counteract damp conditions. So, too, can using cloches to warm the soil up a day or two before sowing. If the soil is too dry water the bottom of the drill, sow the seeds and then cover with dry soil. When sowing in spring you should do so in soil that has been dug and suitably fertilised in autumn or winter. Follow the sowing instructions in this book and on the seed packet as a guide. but bear in mind that weather conditions can make delay advisable. Plants sown a week or two late may do better than those sown when cold and wet.

When sowing try and make you rows as straight as possible — this way you will be making the best use of your plot and when the time comes to thin and hoe you will find life a lot easier. When sowing in summer water the soil well the day before. Always sow thinly — this saves your seed and reduces the need for thinning out later. Cover the drills gently. raking the soil back over and firming down. Don't forget to mark your rows and fill in your planting plan. You may need to protect the seeds from birds. Some seeds can be broadcast — that is to say they can be simply scattered thinly and evenly on the surface. raking first in one direction and then at right angles. This method is particularly useful for sowing early vegetables like carrots. and radishes. cress. lettuce and chicory.

Sowing Indoors

Many plants will benefit from the early start that comes from sowing indoors.

Others need relatively high temperatures to germinate and therefore will always have to be sown indoors or in a warm greenhouse. Both sorts can usually be moved outside once the danger of frosts has passed. Results can be enhanced with the use of an electrically-heated propagator but in most cases you can still germinate most plants either on a window-sill or. for less hardy ones. in an airing cupboard. Plants grown indoors in this fashion will. however. need to be hardened off in a frame or under cloches. This will help them to acclimatise. If you have no frame or cloche then carry them outside for a few mild days. bringing them in at night. before planting out. Always try to sow into sowing or potting compost because garden soil will contain

weed seeds and spores that may damage frail seedlings. Seed composts will nurture your seedlings and provide what they need in the way of nourishment. There are basically two types — loam-based and soil-less. The former type contains sterilised loam. peat. sand and food. The best-known are the John Innes composts which were formulated at the John Innes Horticultural Institute.

Soil-less composts like Levington compost are peat-based with added plant food. They will usually contain enough moisture for sowing but may need extra fertiliser if plants are left in them for more than two or three months.

There is a variety of seed pans and pots available for sowing. Plastic ones are light. easy to clean and cheap. Clay pots give better results and peat pots can be put straight into the ground where the compressed peat simply disintegrates. Make sure your peat pots are very damp when planting and that all other pots are thoroughly washed before re-use.

When sowing into pots or trays fill to the rim and then firm the compost down to about half an inch below. Dribble seeds thinly and evenly allowing up to half an inch between rows of the larger seeds. Cover with a thin layer (about one eighth of an inch) of compost and firm down.

Water lightly. Cover with a sheet of

glass to retain moisture and then a layer of brown paper. Alternatively place in a polythene bag tied tightly at the top. The moment that shoots begin to appear remove coverings. If using a propagator remove the seed tray or pot the moment seedlings appear and place in a warm light place. When the seedlings are large enough to handle they will need to be spread out in other trays or into single pots to give them room to grow. Lift gently and replant in potting compost with the stems covered to a point just below the seed leaves. Water and keep out of direct sunlight for a couple of days. Bear in mind that germination times and temperatures will vary from plant to plant.

Once your plants have grown sturdy and have been hardened off, as described earlier, they can then be transplanted to the growing site or the seedbed. Where possible do your transplanting in mild, damp weather. If the soil is dry give it a good watering the day before planting and water the plants an hour or so beforehand.

Plants in plastic or clay pots should be removed very carefully tapping them out by holding the pot upside down in the palm of your hand with the plant between your fingers.

When your plants have become established you will need to thin out overcrowded rows of those which have been thickly sown like hardy annuals, salad and root vegetables. This will improve growth by reducing competition for light, food and air. A good guide would be to thin first at about one inch high. Single plants should be thinned firstly to about half their final spacing, thinning again later. Take out the weaker plant wherever possible. Water the plants well before thinning allowing any surplus moisture to drain off first.

PLOT

Planning

The essence of producing an efficient and rewarding garden lies in very careful planning. The temptation to start sowing seeds with gay abandon is strong but must be resisted. You will need to give very careful thought not simply to what you are going to grow but to where, when and in what quantity. Do you want a vegetable garden capable of supplying your needs or one which will simply provide some of the more enjoyable seasonal produce? Do you place more importance on a colourful, constantly changing flower garden?

Perhaps you want a mixture of the two. Plan your flowers so that when one group is dying others are emerging to replace them. Think about height, colour and the time of year when they bloom. Don't plant tall flowers in front of short or bushy ones in front of delicate single blooms.

Are you wasting any space?

In the vegetable plot there are plenty of seed grown catch crops that can be schemed in to take advantage of bare patches. Others can be timed so that they occupy space which will later be taken up, say, by brassicas from the seed bed.

Generally speaking you will want your flowers to be visible from the house while the vegetables can be screened off.

These are just a few thoughts to be considered when planning your sowing but individual needs will mean that you may have to consider lots of other factors. The important thing is to plan carefully before sowing.

Soil

You won't grow worthwhile vegetables or flowers unless your soil is fertile. All soil is composed of at least half water and air. The remainder is minerals and organic matter. It is a combination that is never the same in any two gardens but all these components are vital to growth. Mineral elements like sand, silt and clay provide a source of essential nutrients like phosphorus and potash.

The best soil is that which is rich in both nutrients and organic matter, which drains well but which is at the same time moisture retaining. It will have plenty of air holes, worms and a good friable soil structure. It will be either slightly acid or neutral.

If you are less fortunate you may have a very sandy soil which drains rapidly, warms up quickly in spring but is short of nutrients because they are washed out by constant draining. Alternatively you may have a clay soil which form heavy clumps of almost impenetrable soil which becomes very poorly drained, lacks air and stays cold longer.

If your soil lies somewhere in the middle of these two extremes you are lucky but if it corresponds with either description don't despair. A lot can be done to soil to improve it. The key to improving most soils lies in humus — decomposed organic matter. It is packed with nutrients and helps to form a good crumbly soil structure.

Work plenty of it into your soil and it will gradually improve. You won't see dramatic changes overnight but few things of any long term benefit are achieved overnight in a garden.

Organic Matter

Any sort of decomposing vegetation or stable manure will do whether it is garden compost, horse manure, mushroom compost, leaf mould etc.

On lighter soils you will need to use matter that has been well decomposed while on heavier soils a courser grade of material will be needed to help improve the drainage and aeration. As a guide dig in about one full barrow-load for every 25 square feet of soil.

Feeding Your Soil

Organic matter is not usually rich in major plant foods so a balanced fertiliser will usually be needed to promote good, early growth.

Our health conscious world now realises the benefits of a well-balanced diet and the same is true of your soil. In order for your plants to be healthy and long-lived they need a variety of chemicals that come from the soil. Unless you ensure that these are regularly being replaced as they are used up by the plants they may become as unhealthy as you or I if we are deprived of essential vitamins.

The balanced plant diet consists of carbon, hydrogen and oxygen which are absorbed from the atmosphere and the soil plus a number of other nutrients which are taken up, dissolved in water, through the hairs growing near the tips of the plant roots. The three main nutrients are nitrogen, potassium and phosphorus. Nitrogen is important for its ability to promote the growth of leaves and stems. Soil which is rich in nitrogen is ideal for growing plants which are very demanding in their need for nourishment like cabbages, leeks, onions and celery. Nitrogen needs to be replaced in the soil each year through a fertiliser.

Phosphates are important for vigorous root growth. They also help to promote the production of flowers and seeds.

Soil that is rich in phosphates will be ideal for root crops like carrots, turnips, parsnips and swede. Phosphates usually remain in the soil longer than nitrogen — for up to two or three years.

Potassium, more commonly referred to as potash by gardeners, is important in maintaining growth and in helping your plants to resist poor conditions and disease. It helps to build up starches and sugars in vegetable crops particularly potatoes, beetroot and sweet corn.

In addition to these main plant nutrients there is a collection of what are called trace elements that are important for growth. These are zinc, copper, chlorine, molybdenum, magnesium, sulphur, manganese, iron and boron. They are called trace elements because only the merest traces of them are needed — but they are vital all the same.

Finally, your plants will need differing amounts of calcium or lime depending on soil and growing conditions.

So how do you go about providing this vast range of nutrients? Surely you don't need to store all these chemicals individually?

In fact, good farmyard manure will usually provide all you need with the exception of lime. But unfortunately most of us cannot rely on a regular supply of farmyard manure. We will have either to develop our own organic material and add the chemicals or buy some proprietary brand of fertiliser.

As we have explained, organic manure is made up of decaying matter and when it goes into the soil it is converted into plant food by bacteria and fungi. It feeds the soil and the crop with nutrients but it is slow acting. Regular additions of organic manure builds up the soil structure and fertility from year to year.

The commonest organic manures include garden compost, highly nutritious if made properly; farmyard manure, rich and dry but can decay rapidly into a small heap; mushroom compost, good as a garden mulch but contains chalk which may not suit alkaline soils; leaf-mould, alternate layers of leaf and soil adding a little fertiliser to each layer and turn at three month intervals to make a good compost; bonemeal which is ground animal bones and an ideal but slow acting source of phosphates; hoof and horn which is a splendid but

expensive source of nitrogen and, finally, dried blood which is a quick-acting source of nitrogen.

If your soil is excessively acidic or alkaline extra measures may be necessary. Acid soils can be improved by digging in dressings of lime. Soil which is appreciably alkaline, however is more of a problem. You may improve the texture by digging in pulverised bark or acid peat but generally speaking it would be best to grow plants which are tolerant of alkaline soil.

Inorganic Fertilisers

These are generally more quick-acting than organic ones. They feed crops more directly but do not improve your soil. They are usually classed either as compound fertilisers, which provide a balance of the main nutrients, or straight fertilisers which only provide one or two of the nutrients and are used to make up deficiencies or to assist the growth of a particular nutrient-loving plant.

Compound fertilisers contain a balance of the three main nutrients nitrogen, phosphorus and potash and, in addition, minerals such as iron and magnesium. To make your own, mix up 2 lbs. of sulphate of potash, 4 lbs. of sulphate of ammonia, 5 lbs. of superphosphate and apply it at about 2 oz. per square yard.

Straight fertilisers available include: sulphate of potash, ideal for adding potash to soil and safe on all plants. Apply at about 2 oz. per square yard as a top dressing. Nitrate of soda is quick-acting as a source of nitrogen and often used to counteract the checking of plants caused by bad weather.

Apply at 1 oz. per square yard. Sulphate of ammonia can tend to make soil acidic and is best used as part of a compound fertiliser. It supplies nitrogen to the soil and acts within a couple of weeks.

Superphosphate is raked into the soil at up to 4 oz. per square yard and is a relatively slow-acting source of phosphates which will remain in the soil for years. Nitro-chalk is used for acid soils as a source of nitrogen. Top dress at 10 oz. per square yard.

In addition to all of these you can also apply fertilisers in liquid form. They are easily applied as a top dressing and rapidly absorbed by plants. They are usually sold in liquid form but can also be found in solid form. Usually need to be diluted before use.

WEED CONTROL

Weeds compete with your seedlings for water, nutrients and light. The more determined you are about removing them the healthier your plants will be and in some cases it will be advisable to leave your soil fallow to get rid of them thoroughly.

Before sowing anything you will need to have thoroughly weeded your plot. Annual weeds are generally fairly shallow rooting and so can be removed with reasonable ease. Perennials are a bigger problem and if you are not to be plagued by them it would be best to make sure that you have removed and burned them — every trace — before cultivating your site. The alternative is to risk strong and highly invasive perennials like ground elder, couch grass and bindweed taking over. It's not an easy decision to make but eradicating perennials completely is so important in the long run that, if necessary, you should consider delaying planting for a season or more to get the job done. This will not be necessary if you don't have a large problem with perennials but with an overgrown plot then it will have to be considered. Many perennials have such deep roots that digging and weeding may not complete the job. If this is the case — and it will probably be so with vigorous weeds like bindweed — then leave the plot uncultivated and spray in late spring to early summer, when the weeds are growing strongly, with glyphosphate. If there is any re-growth re-spray. It's an arduous and frustrating task but you will be glad you did it.

While your seedlings are growing you will also need to hand weed and hoe. Remove any weeds that appear. If you are very careful you can also spot treat weeds with glyphosphate but be extremely careful not to make contact with any of your seedlings. Chemical treatments have been developed to stop the germination of weed seeds among many plants. One such is lenacil. Another, though with a more restricted range, is simazine. When using any of these products it will be necessary to check with the instructions on the size of the container to see what plants will tolerate its use alongside them. Perhaps a safer method would be to use a mulch between plants avoiding any growing shoots. Suitable mulches include peat, pulverised bark, well-rotted garden compost, leaf mould and mushroom compost. Beware, when using mulches, of importing any new weeds into your garden.

SAVING SEEDS

It is possible to save seeds from your own plants rather than buying them.

However, the exercise can be fraught with problems. First of all you need to be sure you are saving top quality seed. Anything less than good, ripe seed will result in poor crops later on. Secondly, you cannot save the seed of F1, F2 or other hybrids since these usually won't grow the same as the parent plant. You will also have to avoid plants which are inclined to hybridise like members of the cabbage family.

Select plants which set good seed with their own pollen and always save seed from the very best specimens. When beginning save easier seeds like those from tomatoes, beans, marrows, onions, leeks and peas. Try and let the seeds ripen on the plant before collecting them. Remove from the pods, husk or fruit and then clean and dry. Small seeds like foxglove and primula are best sown rapidly after collecting while large seeds like peas should be kept in an envelope in a cool dry place until use.

Tomatoes, marrows and other fruits and berries have obvious seeds which can be scraped out, washed, sieved and dried on a sheet of glass. Small seeds like poppy, statice, pinks etc are best obtained by cutting the whole seed heads when almost ripe, tying them in small bunches and then hanging them upside down in the dry in paper bags. Once they have fully dried store in a cool, airy place or sow immediately. Some plants produce pods which can open up and scatter their seed. To avoid scattering collect the pods before ripening and store in covered jars.

WARNING

All the work and effort you put into growing vegetables and flowers can be totally wasted if the seed is not good. If you are going to save rather than buy commercially-produced seed, you must have total confidence in what you are doing and in the quality of your seed.

LAWNS FROM SEED

Preparing the Site

Before sowing lawn seed a great deal of work will need to have been done in preparing your site. From bare earth in spring or early summer it will need to be graded, if it is not already level, and a drainage system installed if it is needed. In the summer it will need to be dug over to a depth of about nine inches, breaking up clods and digging in lime-free sand if the soil is heavy — peat if it is light. A week or so later the site needs to be firmed down walking all over it with short overlapping steps, treading and raking until it is perfectly firm and level. The soil is then left fallow until you finally prepare it for sowing. Use a long straight plank or step ladder, pulling it across the site to check that it is perfectly level.

Buying Seed

The seed you need to buy will depend on whether you want a luxurious, manicured lawn or one which will survive regular, heavy use. Other factors like whether your site is sunny, shady, wet or damp will also have to be considered. A luxury lawn seed will contain a mixture of fescues and bents. More utilitarian grass seeds contain a blend of course and fine-leaved grasses. Consult fully with your supplier and with the seed packet which should give comprehensive advice and information. It is not worth saving a few pennies at this stage.

SOWING

Choose a day in early or mid-September when the soil is still warm, dry at the top and moist underneath. Don't sow if wet. You can also sow in April but this is going to mean very careful watering throughout the summer especially if it is a dry one. When sowing apply seed at the rate of about $1\frac{1}{2}$ oz. per square yard into soil that has been gently raked to produce very shallow furrows.

Divide the sowing area up into strips and broadcast the seed carefully in each area. Rake in gently to a depth of about one tenth of an inch or cover with finely sifted soil. Rye and meadow grasses take about 14 days to germinate while higher quality grasses can take up to four weeks.

During this time, especially, you will need to protect the seeds from birds. Criss-cross strands of black thread 3–4 ins. above the soil level being very careful not to step on the soil. If rain does not fall for several days you may need to water but this must be done very gently with a very fine rose or fine spray sprinkler. When the grass has reached about 3″ sweep away any stones or worm casts.

Lightly roll it to firm down the soil that has been lifted when the seeds germinated and to encourage the seedlings to develop new shoots. In a few days time the seedlings will have stood up firmly again and it will be time for the first cut. You are aiming to remove only the top half inch of grass and you must have a very sharp blade to do this without tugging at the seedlings. If it is autumn sown no further cutting will be necessary until the spring. If spring-sown you will need to cut regularly, gradually lowering the blade of the mower. A new lawn is a delicate thing and while it may look healthy it should not have any heavy use for a good twelve months after sowing. Water very carefully and keep a close eye out for any weeds or diseases.

HERBS FROM SEED

Outdoors

Most herb seed is sown in early autumn and spring — although some herbs, like chervil, dill and parsley can be sown successively throughout the summer.

Sow in open ground in warm weather when there is no danger of frost. Cover lightly with soil to allow germination. At the four-leaf stage, when seedlings are roughly 2 ins. high thin them out.

Most annual herb seed will germinate taking about two weeks, though parsley will take a lot longer. Many perennial herbs can be grown from seed but will usually take longer to get established. Germination can take up to four weeks.

Indoors

Indoor sowing will give earlier crops. Sow into pots or trays filled with seed compost to within half an inch of the top. Sow thinly and cover with a thin layer of soil. Cover with glass and a sheet of newspaper to keep seeds warm and moist. To germinate properly they will need a temp. of 13°C/58°F. When seedlings have sprouted, in about a week, remove paper and glass and place in the light but not direct sunlight. Keep soil damp. Prick out at the four leaf stage and when well-established harden off and plant out.

TREES AND SHRUBS FROM SEED

The most common methods of raising new trees and shrubs are by division or by layering. Sowing seeds may be relatively easy with flowers and vegetables but with trees and shrubs it can be very difficult for a number of reasons. Germination is fraught with problems, some seeds taking many months and others needing long periods in cold weather to grow. Even when a seedling has become established it can take some years before it has any decorative value in your garden.

There are, however, some which can be raised from seed successfully by the amateur. Among them are Cistus, Genista, Leycesteria and Potentilla. Consult your seedsman or supplier for details of others that can be grown from seed.

The best time for sowing is in the spring. Sow thinly into a pot filled with moist seed and cutting compost. Large seeds will need to be covered with a layer of compost, thin seeds won't. Place the pot inside a polythene bag and seal with an elastic band. Leave the pot in a dark place at a temp. of about 65–70°F. Remove the bag as soon as the seeds have germinated and place them in the light but not direct sunlight. Keep soil moist and turn the pot round to avoid any lop-sided growth. When seedlings are firmly established prick out into pots.

CACTUS FROM SEED

Surprisingly cacti are far easier to raise from seed than you might imagine. Seed should be sown at 18–21°C 65–70°F. Fill well-drained pots with seed compost and sow seeds onto the surface. Cover lightly with silver sand. Cover with glass and shade with newspaper until seedlings appear. Germination can be slow and erratic so don't give up. It may take a month. If seedlings look healthy retain in the pot for the first year. If there are signs of damping-off prick out into small pots.

HOUSE AND GREEN-HOUSE PLANTS

Many flowers and foliage plants can be very successfully grown in the greenhouse or in the home and will give you a supply of pot plants for decoration. Examples of those that can be grown from seed include: Amaryllis, Achimenes, Begonia, Browallia, Campanula, Celosia, Cineraria, Coleus, Cyclamen, Freesia, Gerbera, Gloxinia, Hibiscus, Saintpaulia, Schizanthus and Statice. Even green foliage plants which we associate with more tropical climes can be grown from seed as long as you can give them the heat they need. This will vary from around 21°C to over 30°C depending on the variety.

Those which can successfully be grown by an amateur include the Ficus (Rubber Plant), the Coffea (Coffee Plant) and the Musa (Banana Plant). Buy your seeds from one of the seed merchants which specialise in house and greenhouse seeds like Dobies.

PESTS AND DISEASES

The commonest disease attacking seedlings is damping-off fungus which rots the base of the stem and causes seedlings to collapse and die. Prevent this by watering your compost with a solution of captan, zineb or chestnut compound. Discourage damping-off by sowing thinly and thinning seedlings because overcrowding and stale air can encourage it.

Germinating seeds and seedlings can also be attacked by a variety of soil borne pests and diseases. Seeds can be bought ready dressed with chemical deterrents as we have mentioned earlier. Otherwise a variety of chemicals will have to be used. Discourage the attack of pests and diseases by sowing and transplanting into fresh compost since old stale compost may well harbour spores or fungi. Plants suffering from any disease should be destroyed to prevent it spreading.

FLOWERS FROM SEED

Ageratum
Blue Mink

Ageratums produce blue flowers, in large, tightly packed clusters, from June until the first autumn frosts. The small, compact plants, only 22 cm. (9 ins.) high, are good for bedding, edging, tubs and window boxes.

How to grow: Best in good soil, and in sun or partial shade. They are fairly hardy plants which you sow each year (Half Hardy Annual).
Sow thinly, March/April, in a greenhouse or indoors, using good seed compost. Water compost first, set the seeds and press them lightly into the compost surface. Do not exclude light. Provide 18-21°C. When the second set of leaves appears, transfer seedlings 5 cm. (2 ins.) apart into trays of potting compost. Grow on in good light, then harden them off for example, in a cold frame — before planting out 22 cm. (9 ins.) apart in late May or early June. Set the plants firmly and water well to aid re-establishment.

Alyssum
Saxatile

Produces bright yellow blooms every year. April-June, on low, spreading plants, 25-30 cm. (10-12 ins.) tall and 30-45 cm. (12-18 ins.) across. Best for rockeries, banks or rockery walls.

How to grow: In ordinary, well drained soil where sunny. They are hardy plants and will flower for years (Hardy Perennial).

Outdoors: Sow thinly, May/July, in a seed bed of prepared, moist soil. Cover seeds very lightly with fine soil. When seedlings are 3-5 cm. (1-2 ins.) tall, transfer to where they are to flower next year, or space them 15 cm. (6 ins.) apart in a bed, grow on and plant out 30 cm. (12 ins.) or more apart in flowering positions during autumn.

Under glass: Sow thinly, March/July, in a greenhouse/indoors, using seed compost. Press the seeds lightly into compost surface. Do not exclude light. Provide 13-18°C. When 2nd set of leaves appears, transfer seedlings 5 cm. (2 ins) apart into trays of potting compost. When they have grown big enough to fill the trays, harden them off — for example, in a cold frame — before planting where they are to flower.

Alyssum
Snow Carpet

Masses of tightly packed, pure white, scented flowers on compact plants growing 10-12 cm. (4-5 ins) tall. Flowering June/September. Alyssums are fine for bedding, edging, tubs, window boxes and rockeries.

How to grow: Likes ordinary, well drained garden soil and full sun. Hardy plants which you sow every year (Hardy Annual).

Outdoors: Sow thinly, April/May in prepared, moist soil where they are to flower. Cover seeds very lightly with fine soil. Thin young seedlings to 15 cm. (6 ins.) apart. Surplus seedlings may be transplanted elsewhere.

Under glass: Sow thinly, February/March, in a greenhouse/indoors, using seed compost. Water compost first, set the seeds and press them lightly into the compost surface. Do not exclude light. Provide 13-18°C. When 2nd set of leaves appears, transfer seedlings 5 cm. (2 ins.) apart into trays of potting compost. Grow on in good light, then harden off – for example, in a cold frame – before planting out 20 cm. (8 ins.) apart in late May.

Alyssum
Violet Queen

Compact plants, 15 cm. (6 ins.) tall, with masses of violet coloured, scented flowers, June/September. Very easy to grow and fine for bedding, edging, tubs, window boxes and rockeries.

How to grow: Likes ordinary, well drained garden soil and full sun. Hardy plants which you sow every year (Hardy Annual).

Outdoors: Sow thinly, April/May in prepared, moist soil where they are to flower. Cover seeds very lightly with fine soil. Thin young seedlings to 15 cm. (6 ins.) apart. Surplus seedlings may be transplanted elsewhere.

Under glass: Sow thinly, February/March, in a greenhouse/indoors, using seed compost. Water compost first, set the seeds and press them lightly into the compost surface. Do not exclude light. Provide 13-18°C. When 2nd set of leaves appears, transfer seedlings 5 cm. (2 ins.) apart into trays of potting compost. Grow on in good light, then harden off – for example, in a cold frame – before planting out 20 cm. (8 ins.) apart in late May.

Antirrhinum
Intermediate Mixture

A fine colour mixture of large flowered Snapdragons growing 45-60 cm. (18-24 ins.) tall and blooming from June until October. For beds, borders and tubs.

How to grow: Likes fertile, well drained soil in a sunny position. Fairly hardy plants which you sow every year (Half Hardy Annual).

Outdoors: Sow thinly, April/early May, in warm, moist soil where they are to flower. Cover seeds lightly with fine soil. Thin young seedlings to 25 cm. (10 ins.) apart. Surplus seedlings may be transplanted elsewhere.

Under glass: Sow thinly, February/March, in a greenhouse/indoors, using soilless seed compost. Water compost first, set the seeds and press them lightly into the compost surface. Do not exclude light. Provide 18-21°C. When 2nd set of leaves appears, transfer seedlings 5 cm. (2 ins.) apart into trays of potting compost. Grow on in good light, then harden off – for example, in a cold frame – before planting out 30 cm. (12 ins.) apart in May/early June. When flowers are over, cut away old stems to encourage further blooms. Can also be sown July/Sept.

Antirrhinum
Magic Carpet

A compact growing version of Snapdragon, reaching 20 cm. (8 ins.), for a summer-long display in a wide colour range. For beds, window boxes, tubs and the front of borders.

How to grow: Likes fertile, well drained soil in a sunny position. Fairly hardy plants which you sow every year (Half Hardy Annual).

Outdoors: Sow thinly, April/early May, in warm, moist soil where they are to flower. Cover seeds lightly with fine soil. Thin young seedlings to 20 cm. (8 ins.) apart. Surplus seedlings may be transplanted elsewhere.

Under glass: Sow thinly, February/March, in a greenhouse/indoors, using soilless seed compost. Water compost first, set the seeds and press them lightly into the compost surface. Do not exclude light. Provide 18-21°C. When 2nd set of leaves appears, transfer seedlings 5 cm. (2 ins.) apart into trays of potting compost. Grow on in good light, then harden off – for example, in a cold frame – before planting out 22 cm. (9 ins.) apart in May/early June. When flowers are over, cut away old stems to encourage further blooms. Can also be sown July/Sept.

Aquilegia
Long Spurred Mixture

Columbines grow to 75 cm. (2½ ft.) and flower in May and June, the colourful blooms being graceful, with long spurs, and carried above decorative foliage. Good for garden display and as cut flowers.

How to grow: In rich, well drained soil, and in sun or partial shade. They are hardy plants and will flower for years (Hardy Perennial).

Outdoors: Sow thinly, May/July, in a seed bed of prepared soil. Cover seeds very lightly with fine soil. When 3-5 cm. (1-2 ins.) tall, transfer seedlings to where they are to flower next year, or space them 15 cm. (6 ins.) apart, grow on and plant 40 cm. (15 ins.) apart in flowering positions during autumn.

Under glass: Sow thinly, March/July, in a greenhouse/indoors, using seed compost. Press seeds lightly into compost surface but do not cover. Best to put tray in polythene bag and place in a fridge (0 to 5°C) for 3 weeks. Then, provide 18-21°C. When 2nd set of leaves appears, transfer seedlings 5 cm. (2 ins.) apart into trays. When they have grown big enough to fill the trays, harden off before planting out.

Aster
Andrella

A colour mixture of single and semi-double flowers, that are produced from mid summer into autumn. The plants grow to 60-70 cm. (24-27 ins.) and are excellent for cutting.

How to grow: Asters like well cultivated soil and sun. They are fairly hardy plants which you sow every year (Half Hardy Annual).

Outdoors: Sow thinly, late April/early May, in prepared moist soil where they are to flower. Cover seeds lightly with fine soil. Thin young seedlings to 30-40 cm. (12-15 ins.) apart. Surplus seedlings may be transferred elsewhere.

Under glass: Sow thinly, March/April, in a greenhouse/indoors, using seed compost. Water compost first, set the seeds and cover them lightly with fine compost. Provide 18-21°C. When 2nd set of leaves appears, transfer seedlings 5 cm. (2 ins.) apart into trays of potting compost. Grow in good light, then harden off – for example, in a cold frame – before planting out 40 cm. (15 ins.) apart in late May/early June.

Aster
Ostrich Plume Mixture

These Asters grow 45-60 cm. (18-24 ins.) tall, with large, colourful flowers that are a mass of curled, feathery petals. They bloom from mid summer into the autumn and are fine for beds, borders and as cut flowers.

How to grow: Asters like well cultivated soil and sun. They are fairly hardy plants which you sow every year (Half Hardy Annual).

Outdoors: Sow thinly, late April/ early May, in prepared moist soil where they are to flower. Cover seeds lightly with fine soil. Thin young seedlings to 30-40 cm. (12-15 ins.) apart. Surplus seedlings may be transferred elsewhere.

Under glass: Sow thinly, March/ April, in a greenhouse/indoors, using seed compost. Water compost first, set the seeds and cover them lightly with fine compost. Provide 18-21°C. When 2nd set of leaves appears, transfer seedlings 5 cm. (2 ins.) apart into trays of potting compost. Grow in good light, then harden off – for example, in a cold frame – before planting out 40 cm. (15 ins.) apart in late May/early June.

Aubretia Mixture

Low plants 10 cm. (4 ins.) tall, spreading 30 cm. (12 ins.) or more and having masses of flowers, March/June. Good for rockeries, dry walls and between paving stones. Blooms are violet, lavender, carmine and rose.

How to grow: Best in well drained, slightly limy soil in sun or partial shade. They are hardy plants and will flower for years (Hardy Perennial). Sow thinly, March/July, in a greenhouse/indoors, using seed compost. Press the seeds lightly into the compost surface. Do not exclude light. Provide 13-18°C. When the 2nd set of leaves appears, transfer seedlings 5 cm. (2 ins.) apart into trays of potting compost. When they have grown big enough to fill the trays, harden them off before planting 25-30 cm. (10-12 ins.) apart where they are to flower. Alternatively, move from the trays to individual 8 cm. (3 ins.) pots, and plant out when the pots are nicely filled with roots. After flowering cut back the plants to prevent them from becoming straggly.

Calendula
Fiesta Gitana

Calendulas are one of the easiest of flowers to grow. This sort forms compact plants 30 cm. (12 ins.) tall covered throughout the summer in blooms of orange, tangerine and creamy yellow, and some flowers have a contrasting dark centre. Fiesta Gitana is a Bronze Medal Award winner in the Fleuroselect Trials.

How to grow: Calendulas will grow in most soils though a moist but well drained, moderately fertile soil is best, in a sunny situation. They are hardy plants which you sow each year (Hardy Annual).
Sow thinly, ½ cm. (¼ ins.) deep in prepared, moist soil where the plants are to flower. Thin the young seedlings to 25 cm. (10 ins.) apart. Surplus seedlings may be transplanted elsewhere. To have flowers continuing into autumn, sow several lots of Calendula from the end of March till June. Seeds may also be sown late August/September for earlier flowering the following season. Remove faded blooms to help the plants to flower for as long as possible.

Calendula
Pacific Beauty Mixture

Calendulas are one of the easiest of flowers to grow. This mixture has long stemmed, double flowers throughout the summer in shades of yellow, primrose, apricot and orange. They are good for cutting. The plants grow to 45-60 cm. (1½-2 ft.).

How to grow: Calendulas will grow in most soils though a moist but well drained, moderately fertile soil is best, in a sunny situation. They are hardy plants which you sow each year (Hardy Annual).
Sow thinly, ½ cm. (¼ in.) deep in prepared, moist soil where the plants are to flower. Thin the young seedlings to 30-40 cm. (12-15 ins.) apart. Surplus seedlings may be transplanted elsewhere. To have flowers continuing into autumn, sow several lots of Calendula from the end of March till June. Seeds may also be sown late August/September for earlier flowering the following season. Remove faded blooms to help the plants to flower for as long as possible.

Canary Creeper
Tropaeolum Canariense

This climbing plant can easily grow to 2.4 m. (8 ft.) or more (3.7 m/12 ft.) in one season and it is especially useful for bringing bright colour to walls, fences, pergolas and trellises. The leaves are prettily shaped and the fringed flowers of bright yellow are produced July/October.

How to grow: Best in reasonably fertile soil and in full sun but will also grow in partial shade or in a north facing position. They are hardy plants which you sow each year (Hardy Annual).

Outdoors: Sow in April, ½ cm. (¼ in.) deep, in prepared soil, setting two seeds close together in each position a plant is required. If both germinate, remove the weaker seedling. Plants should be about 90 cm. (3 ft.) apart.

Under glass: For earlier flowers, sow the seeds in March, singly, 5 cm. (2 ins.) apart in trays and provide 13-16°C. Transfer the young plants to individual 8 cm. (3 ins.) pots. Grow on in good light, then harden off — for example, in a cold frame — before planting out in May. Provide twiggy sticks or thin canes to support the plants in the early stages.

Candytuft Fairy Mixture

Produces brightly coloured flowers all through the summer. The plants grow to 20 cm. (8 ins.) in height and they are ideal for borders of low growing plants or as an edging.

How to grow: Candytuft thrives in ordinary, well drained soil and will grow in poor soils. Choose a sunny position. They are hardy plants which you sow each year (Hardy Annual).

Sow thinly, in prepared, moist soil where the plants are to flower. Cover the seeds lightly with fine soil. Thin the young seedlings to 15-20 cm. (6-8 ins.) apart. Surplus seedlings may be transplanted elsewhere. To have flowers continuing through the summer into the autumn, sow several lots of Candytuft from the end of March through to June. Seeds may also be sown late August/September for earlier flowers the following season. Remove faded blooms to help the plants to flower for as long as possible.

Canterbury Bells
Tall Single Mixture

These plants have tall, strong stems with a number of flowers branching out from each. They grow 75 cm. (2½ ft.) high. Colours are blue, mauve, pink and white. Canterbury Bells bloom in June/July.

How to grow: Likes a well cultivated, fertile soil and sun or partial shade. They are hardy plants which you sow one year to flower the next (Hardy Biennial).

Sow thinly, outdoors, in a seed bed of prepared soil during May or June. Cover the seeds very lightly with fine soil. When the seedlings are large enough to handle, transplant them 15-20 cm. (6-8 ins.) apart. Grow on and by late September/October the plants will be ready to plant, 40 cm. (15 ins.) apart, in their flowering positions. To do this, lift the plants carefully to avoid root damage and replant into holes, large enough to accommodate the root system, made with a trowel. Firm the soil around the plants.

Carnation
Annual Mixture

These Carnations have large, beautifully scented double flowers of white and various shades of red, yellow and pink. They grow to 45 cm. (18.ins.), flower from July right into autumn, and they are excellent for bedding and cutting.

How to grow: Carnations like well cultivated, fertile soil with a little lime. Choose a sunny position. They are fairly hardy plants which you sow each year (Half Hardy Annual).

Sow thinly, February/April, in a greenhouse or indoors, using good seed compost. Water the compost, set the seeds and cover them lightly with fine compost. Provide 18-21°C. When the 2nd set of leaves appears, transfer seedlings 5 cm. (2 ins.) apart into trays of potting compost. Grow on in good light, then harden them off — for example, in a cold frame — before planting out 30 cm. (1 ft.) apart in late May or early June. Set the plants firmly and water well to aid re-establishment.

Clarkia
Double Mixture

Clarkias are tall plants, 60-75 cm. (2-2½ ft.) high. Their long stems are encircled with small double flowers from July to September. The colours include red, pink, salmon, carmine, mauve and purple. Ideal for the centre or back of borders and good for cutting.

How to grow: Clarkias like light to medium well drained garden soil in a sunny position or one with light, partial shade. Avoid rich soils which lead to leaf growth at the expense of flowers. They are hardy plants which you sow each year (Hardy Annual).
Sow thinly, in prepared, moist soil where the plants are to flower. Cover the seeds very lightly with fine soil. Thin the young seedlings to 25 cm. (10 ins.) apart. Surplus seedlings may be transplanted elsewhere. Sow the seeds from the end of March to early May. Clarkias can also be sown late August/September for earlier flowers the following season.

Coleus
Rainbow Mixture

Decorative, easily grown foliage pot plants, 40-45 cm. (15-18 ins.) tall, which provide a splash of colour, throughout the year, in a greenhouse/indoors. The leaves are patterned in a wide range of colour combinations.

How to grow: Grow Coleus in potting compost in a greenhouse or on a window sill with full sun but, preferably, give a little shade from summer mid-day sun. Will continue to grow from year to year (Half Hardy Perennial) but, for best results, sow new seeds each year.
Sow thinly, spring/early summer, at 18-21°C in a greenhouse/indoors, using seed compost. Water compost first, set seeds and press them lightly into compost surface. Do not exclude light. When 2nd set of leaves appears, transplant seedlings, individually, to 8 cm. (3 ins.) pots. Later move to 12 cm. (5 ins.) size. When 12 cm. (5 ins.) tall, pinch out the growing tip to induce bushiness. Later, pinching of the side shoots can also be undertaken. Pinch out any flower spikes as they start to form. The seedlings all look alike; the varied colours develop as the plants grow.

Cornflower
Giant Double Blue

These Cornflowers are admired for their true blue colour. The plants reach about 75 cm. (2½ ft.) in height and look best in the middle or back of borders. They make good cut flowers. Cornflowers are easy to grow and they bloom from June to September.

How to grow: Cornflowers grow best in a well drained, fertile soil in a sunny position or one with light, partial shade. They are hardy plants which you sow each year (Hardy Annual). Sow thinly, in prepared, moist soil where the plants are to flower. Cover the seeds lightly with fine soil. Thin the young seedlings to 30 cm. (1 ft.) apart. Surplus seedlings may be transplanted elsewhere. To have flowers continuing into the autumn, sow several lots of Cornflower from the end of March till June. Seeds may also be sown late August/September for earlier flowering the following season. Remove faded blooms to help the plants flower for as long as possible.

Cornflower Polka Dot

Bushy, free flowering plants reaching 40-45 cm. (15-18 ins.) in height. The blooms are produced from June to September and this mixture includes white and various shades of blue, pink and red.

How to grow: Cornflowers grow best in a well drained, fertile soil in a sunny position or one with light, partial shade. They are hardy plants which you sow each year (Hardy Annual). Sow thinly, in prepared, moist soil where the plants are to flower. Cover the seeds lightly with fine soil. Thin the young seedlings to 22 cm. (9 ins.) apart. Surplus seedlings may be transplanted elsewhere. To have flowers continuing into the autumn, sow several lots of Cornflower from the end of March till June. Seeds may also be sown late August/September for earlier flowering the following season. Remove faded blooms to help the plants flower for as long as possible.

Dahlia
Dwarf Double Hybrids

Compact growing, 45-60 cm. (1½-2 ft.) high, with semi-double/double flowers in a wide range of bright colours, from July to the autumn frosts. For beds, borders and cutting.

How to grow: Dahlias like good, fertile soil and sun. Avoid excessive feeding. They are fairly hardy plants and will flower for years (Half Hardy Perennial).
Sow thinly, February/April, in a greenhouse or indoors, using good seed compost. Water compost, set the seeds and cover them lightly with fine compost. Provide 18-21°C. When 2nd set of leaves appears, transfer seedlings 8 cm. (3 ins.) apart into trays of potting compost. Grow in good light, then harden off before planting 40-45 cm. (15-18 ins.) apart in late May/early June. Remove dead blooms to prolong the flowering display. In autumn, after flowering, cut plant stems down to 15 cm. (6 ins.), lift the plants, remove soil from around tubers: store them in slightly moist peat in a frost-proof place. Replant in May. Alternatively, discard plants after flowering and raise new ones each year.

Double Daisy
Large Flowered Mixture

Sturdy and compact plants, just 15 cm. (6 ins.) tall, producing a bright display from April to June, in red, white and pink shades. Good for beds, borders, tubs and window boxes.

How to grow: Double Daisies grow best in fertile, moist soil in sun or partial shade. Avoid hot, dry positions. They are grown as hardy plants which you sow one year to flower the next (Hardy Biennial).
Sow thinly, outdoors, in a seed bed of prepared soil during May or June. Cover the seeds very lightly with fine soil. When the seedlings are large enough to handle, transplant them 10 cm.. (4 ins.) apart. Grow on and by late September/October the plants will be ready to plant, 15 cm. (6 ins.) apart, in their flowering positions. To do this, lift the plants carefully to avoid root damage and replant into holes, large enough to accommodate the root system, made with a trowel. Firm the soil around the plants.

Delphinium
Giant Double Mixture

Tall, graceful plants, ideal for the backs of beds/borders. Growing to 1.5-1.8 m. (5-6 ft.), the stems carry many double and semi-double blooms, June/August. Colours are blue shades, lavender, together with white and some pink.

How to grow: Best in well cultivated, deep, rich soil and in sun. They are hardy plants that flower for years (Hardy Perennial). Keep the seeds cool until required for sowing.

Outdoors: Sow thinly, May/July, in a seed bed of prepared, moist soil. Cover the seeds lightly with fine soil. When 3-5 cm. (1-2 ins.) tall, transplant seedlings 15-20 cm. (6-8 ins.) apart. Grow on and by autumn they will be ready to plant, 75-90 cm. (2½-3 ft.) apart, in their flowering positions.

Under glass: Sow thinly, Feb./July in a greenhouse/indoors, using seed compost. Cover seeds lightly. Provide 18-21°C. When 2nd set of leaves appears, transfer seedlings 8 cm. (3 ins.) apart into trays of potting compost. When they have grown big enough to fill the trays, harden off before planting where they are to flower. Plants from early sowings may flower the same year.

Forget-Me-Not
Myosotis True Blue

Forget-Me-Nots are easy to grow. They bloom April/June and are lovely either as a solid mass of colour or as companions to wallflowers and tulips. Good, too, for tubs and window boxes. The plants grow to 30 cm. (1 ft.) and the blooms are mid-blue in colour.

How to grow: Forget-Me-Nots prefer partial shade and moist soil with a fair amount of organic matter such as peat or garden compost, but they will grow almost anywhere provided the soil is well drained. They are grown as hardy plants which you sow one year to flower the next (Hardy Biennial).
Sow thinly, outdoors, in a seed bed of prepared, moist soil during May or June. Cover the seeds lightly with fine soil. When the seedlings are large enough to handle, transplant them 12 cm. (5 ins.) apart. Grow on and by late September/October the plants will be ready to plant, 25 cm. (10 ins.) apart, in their flowering positions. To do this, lift the plants carefully to avoid root damage and replant into holes, large enough to accommodate the root system, made with a trowel. Firm the soil around the plants.

Geranium
Fine Colour Mixture

The Geranium is a popular pot plant and excellent for summer bedding, for tubs and window boxes. Plants grow to 45-50 cm. (18-20 ins.) and bloom July (or earlier, especially as pot plants) to October, in white and shades of red, pink and salmon.

How to grow: Best in well drained, fertile soil, or in pots of good compost, in a sunny position. Fairly hardy plants which flower for years (Greenhouse/Half Hardy Perennial).

For Outdoors: To bloom 1st summer, sow Dec./Jan., in seed compost: cover seeds lightly. Provide 21-24°C. When 2nd set of leaves appears, transplant, singly into 6cm. (2½ ins.) pots: later, to 9 cm. (3½ ins.) size. Grow in good light: for early flowering, maintain 16-18°C. Harden off before planting out to 30 cm. (1 ft.) apart, late May/early June. Lift early October if to be kept for further year: pot, or plant in boxes of compost.

Pot Plants: Raise as above: may be sown spring/early summer. Final pot size 12 cm. (5 ins.) For all plants, when flowers are over, trim back by a third. In winter, keep just moist: provide 7°C.

Godetia
Dwarf Gem Mixture

Godetias are compact, bushy plants, 30 cm. (12 ins.) in height, with large, densely packed flowers in shades of pink, salmon, carmine and crimson, all through the summer. For beds, borders and window boxes.

How to grow: Godetias will grow in most soils, though a moist but well drained, fairly light soil is best, in a sunny situation. Avoid very rich soils which lead to leaf growth at the expense of flowers. They are hardy plants which you sow each year (Hardy Annual).

Sow thinly, in prepared, moist soil where the plants are to flower. Cover the seeds very lightly with fine soil. Thin young seedlings to 22-25 cm. (9-10 ins.) apart. Surplus seedlings may be transplanted elsewhere. To have flowers continuing through the summer into autumn, sow several lots of Godetia from the end of March through to June. Seeds may also be sown late August/September for earlier flowers the following season. Remove faded blooms to help the plants to flower for as long as possible.

Helichrysum
'Strawflower' Mixture

Versatile, summer blooming plants, 90-120 cm. (3-4 ft.) tall, with brightly coloured flowers. Fine for garden display, for cutting, and dried as 'everlastings' for winter flower arrangements in the home.

How to grow: Best in light, well drained, fertile soil, and in sun. Fairly hardy plants sown each year (Half Hardy Annual).

Outdoors: Sow thinly, late April/ early May, in prepared, moist soil where they are to flower. Cover seeds lightly with fine soil. Thin young seedlings to 40 cm. (15 ins.) apart.

Under glass: Sow thinly, March/ April, in a greenhouse/indoors, using seed compost. Press seeds lightly into compost surface. Do not exclude light. Provide 18-21°C. When 2nd set of leaves appears, transfer seedlings 5 cm. (2 ins.) apart into trays of potting compost. Grow in good light, then harden off — for example, in a cold frame — before planting out in late May/early June. Cut the flowers for winter decoration before they are fully open and showing the central disc. To dry, tie in bunches and hang them upside down in a cool, airy place out of the sun.

Impatiens
Dwarf Mixture

Superb for summer bedding, for tubs, window boxes and hanging baskets, and also as pot plants. Good for both sun and shade, they grow 15-20 cm. (6-8 ins.) high. Produce masses of small, open flowers — June/ October, when bedded out — in white, and shades of pink, salmon, carmine, lilac, orange and scarlet.

How to grow: Impatiens like fertile, moist, but well drained soil in sun or shade. Fairly hardy plants that can be grown from year to year (Half Hardy Perennial), you get far better results by sowing new seeds each year.

For Outdoors: Sow thinly, Feb./ March, in a greenhouse/indoors. Press seeds lightly into seed compost surface. Do not exclude light. Provide 21-24°C. When 2nd set of leaves appears, transfer seedlings 5 cm. (2 ins.) apart into trays of potting compost. Grow in good light, then harden off before planting out, 22 cm. (9 ins.) apart, late May/early June.

Pot Plants: Sow as above, through to early summer but move seedlings, singly, to 6 cm. (2½ ins.) pots: later, transfer to larger pots (final size 11-12 cm./4½-5 ins.). Grown this way, flowering may continue most of the year round.

Lobelia
String of Pearls Mixture

These Lobelias have a wide colour range — light and dark blue, red, rosy carmine, white and purple. They form bushy plants, 15 cm. (6 ins.) high, covered in a mass of small flowers — from June through to autumn frosts — so that few leaves are visible. For tubs and window boxes, as edging or between paving stones.

How to grow: Lobelias like rich, moist but well drained soil in sun or light, partial shade. They are fairly hardy plants which you sow each year (Half Hardy Annual).
Sow thinly, February/March, in a greenhouse or indoors, using good seed compost. Water compost first, set the seeds and press them lightly into the compost surface. Do not exclude light. Provide 18-21°C. The seedlings that appear are very small. When the 2nd set of leaves appears, transfer the seedlings, in groups of 3-4, 5 cm. (2 ins.) apart into trays of potting compost. Grow in good light, then harden off — for example, in a cold frame — before planting out, 10-15 cm. (4-6 ins.) apart, late May/early June.

Lobelia
Compact Dark Blue

Produces masses of small, deep blue flowers, June through to autumn frosts. The spreading plants grow 15 cm. (6 ins.) tall. Ideal for edging and most effective mixed with white Alyssum. Good, too, for tubs, window boxes, hanging baskets and between paving stones.

How to grow: Lobelias like rich, moist but well drained soil in sun or light, partial shade. They are fairly hardy plants which you sow each year (Half Hardy Annual).
Sow thinly, February/March, in a greenhouse or indoors, using good seed compost. Water compost first, set the seeds and press them lightly into the compost surface. Do not exclude light. Provide 18-21°C. The seedlings that appear are very small. When the 2nd set of leaves appears, transfer the seedlings, in groups of 3-4, 5 cm. (2 ins.) apart into trays of potting compost. Grow in good light, then harden off — for example, in a cold frame — before planting out, 10-15 cm. (4-6 ins.) apart, late May/early June. Lobelias look good in window boxes with Nemesias.

Lobelia
Pendula Sapphire

This variety produces long trailing stems, dotted with rich blue, white-eyed blooms from June through to the autumn frosts. The trailing habit of growth makes it ideal for hanging baskets, tubs, window boxes and for growing down banks and walls.

How to grow: Lobelias like rich, moist but well drained soil in sun or light, partial shade. They are fairly hardy plants which you sow each year (Half Hardy Annual).
Sow thinly, February/March, in a greenhouse or indoors, using good seed compost. Water compost first, set the seeds and press them lightly into the compost surface. Do not exclude light. Provide 18-21°C. The seedlings that appear are very small. When the 2nd set of leaves appears, transfer the seedlings, in groups of 3-4, 5 cm. (2 ins.) apart into trays of potting compost. Grow in good light, then harden off — for example, in a cold frame — before planting out, 10-15 cm. (4-6 ins.) apart, late May/early June. Trailing Lobelias look lovely in hanging baskets with Nasturtiums.

Lupin
Russell Strain

Lupins grow 90-110 cm. (3-3½ ft.) tall with ornamental foliage and many small flowers, closely packed around upright stems, May/July. The wide colour range includes some blooms with attractive two-tone effects.

How to grow: Likes ordinary, well drained soil in sun/partial shade. Avoid over-rich conditions or limy soils for best results. They are hardy plants and will flower for years (Hardy Perennial).

Outdoors: Soak seeds in warm water for 24 hours before sowing 5 cm. (2 ins.) apart, May/July, in a seed bed of prepared soil. Cover seeds lightly. When 5 cm. (2 ins.) tall, transfer seedlings to where they are to flower next year, or space them 15 cm. (6 ins.) apart, grow on and plant 50-60 cm. (20-24 ins.) apart during autumn.

Under glass: Soak seeds as above. Sow 5 cm. (2 ins.) apart, Feb./July, in greenhouse/indoors, using seed compost. Cover seeds lightly. Provide 16-18°C. When young plants have grown big enough to fill the trays, harden them off before planting out. Plants from greenhouse sowings in Feb. may flower the same year.

African Marigold
Crackerjack

These African Marigolds produce large, round flowers of primrose, yellow, gold and orange late June/October, on sturdy plants 75-90 cm. (2½-3 ft.) high. For beds, borders and as cut flowers.

How to grow: African Marigolds will grow in most well cultivated soils, but a moderately fertile soil is best, in a sunny situation. They are fairly hardy plants which you sow each year (Half Hardy Annual).

Sow thinly, February/early April, in a greenhouse or indoors, using good seed compost. Water compost first, set the seeds and cover them lightly with fine compost. Provide 18-21°C. When the 2nd set of leaves appears, transfer seedlings 5 cm. (2 ins.) apart into trays of potting compost. Grow in good light, then harden off — for example, in a cold frame — before planting out 45 cm. (18 ins.) apart in late May/early June. Remove dead blooms to prolong the flowering display.

French Marigold
Double Colour Magic

Compact bushy plants, growing to 20-25 cm. (8-10 ins.) in height and producing double flowers, June/October, in a range of red and gold shades including bicoloured types. Ideal for beds, tubs and window boxes.

How to grow: French Marigolds will grow in most well cultivated soils, but a moderately fertile soil is best, in a sunny position. They are fairly hardy plants which you sow each year (Half Hardy Annual).

Outdoors: Sow thinly, May/early June, in prepared moist soil where they are to flower. Cover seeds lightly. Thin young seedlings to 22 cm. (9 ins.) apart. Surplus seedlings may be transferred elsewhere.

Under glass: Sow thinly, March/April, in a greenhouse/indoors, using seed compost. Water compost first, set the seeds and cover them lightly. Provide 18-21°C. When the 2nd set of leaves appears, transfer seedlings 5 cm. (2 ins.) apart into trays of potting compost. Grow in good light, then harden off before planting out, late May/early June. Remove dead blooms to prolong the flowering display.

French Marigold
Petite Mixture

Produces numerous flowers that resemble tiny, rounded powder puffs. Petite Marigolds, 15 cm. (6 ins.) tall, are perfect for bedding, edging, tubs and window boxes. They bloom June/October with flowers in shades of orange, gold, yellow and mahogany red.

How to grow: Will grow in most well cultivated soils, but a moderately fertile soil is best, in a sunny position. Fairly hardy plants sown each year (Half Hardy Annual).

Outdoors: Sow thinly, May/early June, in prepared moist soil where they are to flower. Cover seeds lightly. Thin young seedlings to 20 cm. (8 ins.) apart. Surplus seedlings may be transferred elsewhere.

Under glass: Sow thinly, March/April, in a greenhouse/indoors, using seed compost. Water compost first, set the seeds and cover them lightly. Provide 18-21°C. When the 2nd set of leaves appears, transfer seedlings 5 cm. (2 ins.) apart into trays of potting compost. Grow in good light, then harden off before planting out, late May/early June. Remove dead blooms to prolong the flowering display.

Mesembryanthemum
Criniflorum Mixture

Masses of daisy-like flowers, in a wide range of glistening colours, from June until September, on plants just 8 cm. (3 ins.) high. For rock gardens, banks or the edges of borders — also tubs and window boxes.

How to grow: Will grow in any well-drained soil, including light, dry soils. Full sun required. They are fairly hardy plants which you sow each year (Half Hardy Annual).
Sow thinly, February/March, in a greenhouse or indoors, using good seed compost. Water compost first, set the seeds and press them lightly into the compost surface. Do not cover the seeds with compost but place seed tray in a dark place or cover it to exclude light, until seedlings appear. Provide 18-21°C. When the 2nd set of leaves appears, transfer seedlings 8 cm. (3 ins.) apart into trays of potting compost. Grow on in good light, then harden them off — for example, in a cold frame — before planting out 25 cm. (10 ins.) apart in late May or early June. Removal of faded blooms helps to prolong the flowering display.

Morning Glory
Heavenly Blue

True blue, trumpet shaped blooms —
up to 12 cm. (5 ins.) across and produced July/September — which open
in the mornings and fade during the
afternoon. Growing to 2.4 m. (8 ft.) or
more, the plants have twining stems
and heart shaped leaves. For a fence,
trellis, wall, a tripod of canes or in
pots.

How to grow: Likes a light, well
drained, fertile soil in a sunny, sheltered position. Avoid very rich soils.
Fairly hardy plants sown each year
(Half Hardy Annual).
Soak seeds in warm water for 24
hours before sowing, March/April in
a greenhouse/indoors, 1 seed to an
8 cm. (3 ins.) pot of seed compost.
Cover seeds lightly. Provide 20-24°C.
Use thin canes for initial support.
Harden off before planting out 30 cm.
(1 ft.) apart, late May/early June,
when weather is warm. For greenhouse, move to 11-12 cm. (4½-5 ins.)
pots when small ones are filled with
roots. (May also be needed for early
raised plants for outdoors). Later,
transfer to 15-18 cm. (6-7 ins.) pots.
Provide support for plants. In pots,
stems can be trained around frame-
work of canes to prevent plants
becoming too tall.

Nasturtium
Dwarf Jewel Mixture

These plants will grow in almost any
poor, dry soil. They are 22-30 cm.
(9-12 ins.) tall and ideal for beds,
edging, window boxes, tubs, hanging
baskets and children's gardens. The
semi-double flowers, produced June
to September, are in shades of
yellow, orange-scarlet, salmon and
mahogany red. The young leaves
have a peppery taste and can be
used in salads.

How to grow: Nasturtiums thrive in
poor or ordinary, dry soil with plenty of
sun. Avoid rich soils which encourage
foliage at the expense of flowers.
They are hardy plants which you sow
each year (Hardy Annual).
Sow the seeds 1 cm. (½ in.) deep and
12-15 cm. (5-6 ins.) apart, mid April/
May, in prepared, moist soil where
the plants are to flower. Thin young
seedlings to 24-30 cm. (10-12 ins.)
apart. Surplus seedlings may be
transplanted elsewhere, avoiding
root disturbance as far as possible.
Nasturtiums look lovely in hanging
baskets — for example, with trailing
Lobelias. For baskets, sow seeds
singly, February/March, in 8 cm. (3
ins.) pots filled with seed compost.
Provide 13-16°C.

Nasturtium
Empress of India

A striking variety with bluish-green leaves, and trumpet shaped flowers of crimson-scarlet, June/September. The plants grow 22 cm. (9 ins.) tall and are ideal for beds, edgings, window boxes, tubs, hanging baskets and children's gardens. Good subjects for poor, dry soils where other plants may find it difficult to grow. The young leaves have a peppery pungency and can be used in salads.

How to grow: Nasturtiums thrive in poor or ordinary, dry soil with plenty of sun. Avoid rich soils which encourage foliage at the expense of flowers. They are hardy plants which you sow each year (Hardy Annual).
Sow the seeds 1 cm. (½ in.) deep and 12-15 cm. (5-6 ins.) apart, mid April/May, in prepared, moist soil where the plants are to flower. Thin young seedlings to 24-30 cm. (10-12 ins.) apart. Surplus seedlings may be transplanted elsewhere, avoiding root disturbance as far as possible. Nasturtiums look lovely in hanging baskets — for example, with trailing Lobelias. For baskets, sow seeds singly, February/March, in 8 cm. (3 ins.) pots filled with seed compost. Provide 13-16°C.

Nasturtium
Giant Climbing Mixture

A vigorous variety that can be trained up trellises, fences or tree trunks — the plants reaching up to 3 m. (10 ft.) — or left to ramble down garden banks. The single flowers, produced from June to September, come in shades of crimson, scarlet, orange and yellow. Nasturtiums produce a wealth of colour on poor, dry soils where other plants may find it difficult to grow. The young leaves have a peppery pungency and can be used in salads.

How to grow: Nasturtiums thrive in poor or ordinary, dry soil with plenty of sun. Avoid rich soils which encourage foliage at the expense of flowers. They are hardy plants which you sow each year (Hardy Annual).
Sow the seeds 1 cm. (½ in.) deep and 15 cm. (6 ins.) apart, mid April/May, in prepared moist soil where the plants are to flower. Thin the young seedlings to 30-45 cm. (12-18 ins.) apart. Surplus seedlings may be transplanted elsewhere, avoiding root disturbance as far as possible.

Nasturtium
Gleam Hybrids

Semi-double flowers, produced June/September, in shades of yellow, gold, orange, salmon, orange-scarlet and crimson on 30 cm. (1 ft.) tall plants of semi-trailing habit. Particularly good for hanging baskets: ideal for beds, window boxes, tubs and children's gardens. They produce a wealth of colour on poor, dry soils. The young leaves have a peppery taste and can be used in salads.

How to grow: Nasturtiums thrive in poor or ordinary, dry soil with plenty of sun. Avoid rich soils which encourage foliage at the expense of flowers. They are hardy plants which you sow each year (Hardy Annual).
Sow the seeds 1 cm. (½ in.) deep and 15 cm. (6 ins.) apart, mid April/May, in prepared, moist soil where the plants are to flower. Thin young seedlings to 30-45 cm. (12-18 ins.) apart. Surplus seedlings may be transplanted elsewhere, avoiding root disturbance as far as possible. Nasturtiums look lovely in hanging baskets — for example, with trailing Lobelias. For baskets, sow seeds singly, February/March, in 8 cm. (3 ins.) pots filled with seed compost. Provide 13-16°C.

Nasturtium
Whirlybird Mixture

Nasturtium Whirlybird flowers do not have the usual spur behind the petals. The blooms are upward facing and they are carried above the foliage on plants 15 cm. (6 ins.) tall. Colours include shades of mahogany, scarlet, rosy red, cherry, orange, gold and cream. They will grow in almost any poor, dry soil. The young leaves have a peppery taste and can be used in salads.

How to grow: Nasturtiums thrive in poor or ordinary, dry soil with plenty of sun. Avoid rich soils which encourage foliage at the expense of flowers. They are hardy plants which you sow each year (Hardy Annual).
Sow 1 cm. (½ in.) deep and 12-15 cm. (5-6 ins.) apart, mid April/May, in prepared, moist soil where the plants are to flower. Thin young seedlings to 24-30 cm. (10-12 ins.) apart. Surplus seedlings may be transplanted elsewhere, avoiding root disturbance as far as possible. Nasturtiums look lovely in hanging baskets — for example, with trailing Lobelias. For baskets, sow seeds singly, February/March, in 8 cm. (3 ins.) pots filled with seed compost. Provide 13-16°C.

Nemesia
Carnival Mixture

Bushy plants, 25 cm. (10 ins.) high, each one a mass of flowers. They bloom from June until September in a very wide range of most attractive colours. Nemesias look best massed in beds, borders, tubs or window boxes.

How to grow: Nemesias like fertile, moist but well drained soil and full sun. They are fairly hardy plants which you sow each year (Half Hardy Annual).

Outdoors: Sow thinly, late May/early June, in prepared, moist soil where they are to flower. Cover the seeds lightly. Thin young seedlings to 10-15 cm. (4-6 ins.) apart. Surplus seedlings may be transferred elsewhere.

Under glass: Sow thinly, March/April, in a greenhouse/indoors, using seed compost. Cover seeds lightly. Exclude light until seedlings start to appear. Provide 16-21°C. When 2nd set of leaves appears, transfer seedlings 5 cm. (2 ins.) apart into trays of potting compost. Grow in good light, then harden off before planting out, 12-15 cm. (5-6 ins.) apart, late May/early June. Pinch out growing tip when the plants are 8 cm. (3 ins.) tall. Water well in dry weather.

Nicotiana
Tinkerbell

Fragrant, star shaped, trumpet-like flowers of crimson, red, pink, rose, yellowish-green and white, produced June to September, on bushy plants 30 cm. (1 ft.) in height. Superb for beds, borders and tubs.

How to grow: Nicotianas like a rich, moist but well drained soil and full sun. They are fairly hardy plants which you sow each year (Half Hardy Annual).

Sow thinly, mid February/April, in a greenhouse or indoors, using good seed compost. Water the compost first, set the seeds and press them lightly into the compost surface. Do not exclude light. Provide 20-24°C. When the second set of leaves appears, transfer seedlings 5 cm. (2 ins.) apart into trays of potting compost. Grow on in good light, then harden them off — for example, in a cold frame — before planting out 25 cm. (10 ins.) apart in late May or early June. Set the plants firmly and water well to aid re-establishment.

Pansy
Choice Mixture

These Pansies, grow 15-20 cm. (6-8 ins.) tall and have flowers of velvety appearance, in a wide range of lovely colours, from May to September. Excellent for beds, borders, tubs, window boxes and as cut flowers.

How to grow: Pansies like fertile, moist but well drained soil in sun or partial shade. They are hardy plants and will flower for years (Hardy Perennial) but, for best results, sow new seeds each year.

Outdoors: Sow thinly, mid March/April, in prepared moist soil where they are to flower. Cover seeds lightly with fine soil. Thin young seedlings to 20 cm. (8 ins.) apart. Surplus seedlings may be transferred elsewhere

Under glass: Sow thinly February/early April, in a greenhouse/indoors, using seed compost. Cover seeds lightly with fine compost. Exclude light until seedlings start to appear. Provide 18-21°C. When 2nd set of leaves appears, transfer seedlings 5 cm. (2 ins.) apart into trays of potting compost. Grow in good light, then harden off before planting out, 22-25 cm. (9-10 ins.) apart, May/early June. Remove faded blooms to prolong the flowering display.

Pansy
Winter Flowering Mixture

These Pansies, 15-20 cm. (6-8 ins.) tall, flower in mild weather from late autumn, through winter to early spring, giving a wealth of colour when there is little to be had. Perfect for beds, tubs and window boxes. The colours are yellow, orange, violet, blue, red, bronze and white, some blooms being whiskered or with dark blotches.

How to grow: Winter Pansies like fertile, well drained soil and sun or light, partial shade. They are hardy plants and will flower for years (Hardy Perennial) but, for best results, sow new seeds each year.
Sow thinly, May/July, in a seed bed of prepared soil. Cover seeds lightly. When 3-5 cm. (1-2 ins.) tall, transplant seedlings 10 cm. (4 ins.) apart. Grow on and by late September/October plant out, 20 cm. (8 ins.) apart, in their flowering positions. Alternatively, sow in a seed tray placed in a cold frame. When 2nd set of leaves appears, transfer seedlings 5 cm. (2 ins.) apart into trays of compost. Grow on in frame/outdoors and plant out in autumn. Remove faded blooms to prolong the flowering display.

Petunia
Fine Mixture

Petunias give a superb display from June through to the autumn frosts. The trumpet shaped flowers, in pink, rose, red, purple, dark blue and white, are produced on plants 30 cm. (12 ins.) tall. Excellent for beds, borders, hanging baskets, tubs and window boxes.

How to grow: Likes reasonably fertile, well drained soil and sun. Avoid over-rich soils which encourage foliage at the expense of flowers. They are fairly hardy plants which you sow each year (Half Hardy Annual).
Sow thinly, February/April, in a greenhouse or indoors, using seed compost. Water compost first, set the seeds and press them lightly into the compost surface. Do not exclude light. Provide 18-21°C. When 2nd set of leaves appears, transplant seedlings 5 cm. (2 ins.) apart into trays of potting compost. Grow in good light, then harden off — for example, in cold frame — before planting out 30 cm. (12 ins.) apart in late May/early June. Pinch out growing tip when 12 cm. (5 ins.) tall. Remove faded blooms to prolong flowering display. Petunias look lovely in window boxes with trailing Lobelias.

Polyanthus
Superb Mixture

Splendid for an eye-catching spring display — March to May. Polyanthus grow 25-30 cm. (10-12 ins.) tall and the colourful blooms are produced in clusters on sturdy, upright stems. Ideal for beds, borders, edging or in pots.

How to grow: Likes moist, fertile soil and sun or partial shade. They are hardy plants which flower for years (Hardy Perennial).
Sow thinly, March/July, in a greenhouse, frame or indoors, using seed compost. Press seeds lightly into compost surface. Tray can be put in polythene bag and placed in a fridge (0 to 5°C) for 3-4 weeks to assist germination which may be slow/erratic. After chilling period, provide 16-18°C. Do not exclude light. When 2nd set of leaves appears, transfer seedlings 5 cm. (2 ins.) apart into trays of potting compost. Grow cool and, with early raised plants, when trays are well filled with roots, transfer plants 10 cm. (4 ins.) apart, outdoors. In all cases, plant out, September/October, 22 cm. (9 ins.) apart.

Pot plants: Transfer from growing-on tray to individual 9 cm. (3½ ins.) pots for cool greenhouse/home display.

Californian Poppy
Colour Mixture

Every part of the Californian Poppy — leaf, stem and flower - is delicately formed and adds a touch of elegance to beds and borders. Bright, showy plants, with a wide colour range, they flower June to October and reach 30 cm. (1 ft.) in height. Easy to grow and ideal for children's gardens.

How to grow: Likes ordinary, well drained soil and full sun. Will grow in poor soils, not requiring rich conditions. It is a hardy plant which you sow each year (Hardy Annual).
Sow thinly, in prepared, moist soil where the plants are to flower. Cover the seeds lightly with fine soil. Thin the young seedlings to 15-20 cm. (6-8 ins.) apart. Surplus seedlings may be transplanted elsewhere, avoiding root disturbance as far as possible. To have flowers continuing through the summer into the autumn, sow several lots of seed from the end of March till June. Seeds may also be sown late August/September for earlier flowering the following season. Remove faded blooms to help the plants to flower for as long as possible.

Rudbeckia
Rustic Dwarfs

Large, daisy-like flowers in rich shades of golden bronze, chestnut, mahogany and yellow, with a contrasting dark, central cone. The bushy plants, 45-55 cm. (18-22 ins.) tall, bloom July/October and are superb for beds and borders. Excellent cut flowers, too. 'Rustic Dwarfs' is a Bronze Medal Award winner in the All Britain Trials.

How to grow: Rudbeckias like reasonably fertile, well drained soil and sun. They are fairly hardy plants which you sow each year (Half Hardy Annual).
Sow thinly, February/March, in a greenhouse/indoors, using seed compost. Cover the seeds lightly with fine compost. Provide 18-21°C. When 2nd set of leaves appears, transfer seedlings 8 cm. (3 ins.) apart into trays of potting compost. Grow in good light, then harden off — for example, in a cold frame — before planting out 40-45 cm. (15-18 ins.) apart in late May/early June. To prolong cut flower life, dip bottom 2 cm. (1 in.) of stem in boiling water for 30 seconds, immediately after cutting.

Salvia
Blaze of Fire

Salvias bloom from July through to the first autumn frost. The brilliant scarlet flowers are tubular in shape and massed all around the stems. They are compact plants, 30 cm. (1 ft.) tall, and excellent for beds and borders.

How to grow: Salvias like fertile, well drained soil and full sun. They are fairly hardy plants which you sow each year (Half Hardy Annual).
Sow thinly, February/March, in a greenhouse or indoors, using good seed compost. Water compost first, set the seeds and press them lightly into the compost surface. Do not exclude light. Provide 18-21°C. When 2nd set of leaves appears, transfer seedlings 5 cm. (2 ins.) apart into trays of potting compost. Grow on in good light, then harden them off — for example, in a cold frame — before planting out 30 cm. (1 ft.) apart in late May or early June. Set the plants firmly and water well to aid re-establishment. Pinch out the growing tip. when the plants are 8 cm. (3 ins.) tall, to encourage a bushy habit.

Schizanthus
'Butterfly Flower' Mixture

Schizanthus nave clusters of orchid-like flowers — in shades of red, rose, pink, lavender, and white — prettily veined and marked with contrasting colours. They are produced June/October on plants growing 40-45 cm. (15-18 ins.) high and having attractive fern-like leaves. For beds, borders and window boxes.

How to grow: Schizanthus like a moist, but well drained, fertile soil in a sheltered, sunny position. They are fairly hardy plants which you sow each year (Half Hardy Annual).

Outdoors: Sow thinly, late April/early May, in prepared moist soil where they are to flower. Cover seeds very lightly. Thin young seedlings to 25-30 cm. (10-12 ins.) apart. Surplus seedlings may be transferred elsewhere.

Under glass: Sow thinly, March/early April, in greenhouse/indoors, using seed compost. Press seeds lightly into surface. Place seed tray in a dark place or cover it to exclude light until seedlings appear. Provide 16-18°C. When 2nd set of leaves appears, transfer seedlings 5 cm. (2 ins.) apart into trays of potting compost. Grow in good light, then harden off before planting out, late May/early June, 30 cm. (1 ft.) apart.

Statice
Pacific Mixture

Produces winged stems carrying clusters of flowers in deep rose, peach, yellow, blue, rosy lavender, delicate pink and white. Statice blooms July to September and the plants grow to 45-60 cm. (1½-2 ft.). For beds and borders, as cut flowers and dried as 'everlastings' for winter floral arrangements in the home.

How to grow: In ordinary, well drained soil where sunny. They are fairly hardy plants which you sow each year (Half Hardy Annual).
Sow thinly, February/March, in a greenhouse/indoors using seed compost. Cover the seeds lightly with fine compost. Provide 18-21°C. When 2nd set of leaves appears, transplant seedlings 5 cm. (2 ins.) apart into trays of potting compost. Grow in good light, then harden off — for example, in a cold frame — before planting out 30 cm. (1 ft.) apart in late May/early June. Cut the flowers for winter decoration when they are well coloured but not fully opened or mature. Tie in bunches and hang them upside down in a cool, airy place out of the sun.

Brompton Stock
Spring Flowering Stock

Brompton Stocks have superb, double and single flowers with a heavy scent and a wide range of colours. They flower in May/June, the blooms being tightly packed around stems that grow to 45 cm. (1½ ft.) in height. For beds, borders and as cut flowers.

How to grow: Brompton Stocks like fertile, well drained soil with a little lime. Choose a warm, sheltered position in full sun. They are hardy plants which you sow one year to flower the next (Hardy Biennial).
Sow thinly, outdoors in a seed bed of prepared soil, June/July. Cover the seeds lightly with fine soil. When the seedlings are large enough to handle, transplant them 15 cm. (6 ins.) apart. Grow on and by late September/October the plants will be ready to plant 30 cm. (1 ft.) apart, in their flowering positions. Except for mild, sheltered areas, it is better to transplant seedlings into a cold frame, to 9 cm. (3½ ins.) pots to plunge in a frame, or to where they can be covered by cloches during cold winter weather. Plant out in March where they are to flower.

Night Scented Stock

This summer flowering Stock opens its lilac/pink blooms at night, when its heady scent floats on the air. Sow near your windows to enjoy the fragrance coming in on summer evenings. Night Scented Stock is a bushy plant, 22-30 cm. (9-12 ins.) tall, with 4-petalled flowers and narrow, grey-green leaves. As the flowers are shut during the day, and so a bit dull, it is a good idea to mix the seeds with those of Virginian Stock, to give you plenty of day-time colour.

How to grow: Night Scented Stocks will grow in ordinary garden soil and do not need full sun. They are hardy plants which you sow each year (Hardy Annual).
So thinly, in prepared, moist soil where the plants are to flower. Cover the seeds lightly with fine soil. Thin the young seedlings to 10-12 cm. (4-5 ins.) apart. Surplus seedlings may be transplanted elsewhere. To have flowers continuing through the summer into autumn, sow several lots of seeds from the end of March until June. These Stocks grow well in window boxes. Mix them with Virginian Stock, for fragrance as well as colour.

Ten Week Stock
Dwarf Finest Mixture

These Stocks grow 30-40 cm. (12-15 ins.) tall, the stems covered with closely packed double or single flowers that begin to open ten weeks after sowing — hence their name. The scented flowers are produced June to September and come in crimson, pink, rose, cream, mid blue, purple, appleblossom and white.

How to grow: Likes fertile, well drained soil with a little lime, and sun or partial shade. It is a plant which you sow each year (Half Hardy Annual).

Outdoors: Sow thinly, late April/early May in prepared moist soil where they are to flower. Cover the seeds very lightly. Thin young seedlings to 25 cm. (10 ins.) apart. Surplus seedlings may be transferred elsewhere.

Under glass: Sow thinly, March/April, in a greenhouse/indoors, using seed compost. Press the seeds lightly into the surface. Do not exclude light. Provide 18-21°C. When 2nd set of leaves appears, transfer seedlings 5 cm. (2 ins.) apart into trays of potting compost. Grow in good light, then harden off before planting out, 25-30 cm. (10-12 ins.) apart, in late May/early June.

Virginian Stock
Finest Mixture

Virginian Stocks produce a mass of four petalled flowers, on slender stems, in white and shades of lilac, rose and red. The plants are bushy, 22 cm. (9 ins.) high, very easy to grow, and they bloom during the summer. For beds, borders, edging, and children's gardens.

How to grow: Virginian Stocks will grow in most soils and positions but an open, sunny situation is best. They are hardy plants which you sow each year (Hardy Annual).
Sow thinly, in prepared, moist soil where the plants are to flower. Cover the seeds lightly with fine soil. Thin the young seedlings to 8 cm. (3 ins.) apart. Surplus seedlings may be transplanted elsewhere. To have flowers continuing through the summer into autumn, sow several lots of seeds from the end of March until July. Virginian Stocks grow well in window boxes. Mix them with Night Scented Stocks for fragrance as well as colour.

Sunflower
Tall Single

These Sunflowers produce blooms, up to 30 cm. (1 ft.) or more across, of golden-yellow with contrasting dark centre, from late July to September. They easily reach 2.2-2.8 m. (7-9 ft.) in height and, with extra care, can grow to 4.3 m. (14 ft.) or even more.

How to grow: Sunflowers will grow in well drained, ordinary garden soil, in full sun. They are hardy plants which you sow each year (Hardy Annual).
Sow late March to May, ½ cm. (¼ in.) deep, in prepared soil, setting 2-3 seeds close together in each position a plant is required, thinning to 1 seedling when they are 3-5 cm. (1-2 ins.) tall. Plants should be 60 cm. (2 ft.) apart — but for really tall ones, allow 1.2-1.5 m. (4-5 ft.). Support the plants by tying them to stout canes or stakes. If you want Sunflowers to grow as high as possible, dig the soil well and add some rotted manure before sowing. Choose a really sunny position and keep the plants well watered during the summer. Feed them regularly with a liquid general fertiliser.

Sweet Pea
Giant Waved

Beautifully scented flowers, with large wavy petals, in a wide colour range. Fine for garden display and excellent for cutting. The more you pick them, the more they bloom from June through to September. The plants climb to 1.8 m. (6 ft.) or more and should be trained up a trellis, netting, or use twiggy sticks or canes and twine.

How to grow: Best in rich, well drained soil with a little lime, and in full sun. They are hardy plants sown each year (Hardy Annual).

Outdoors: Soak seeds in water for 12 hours before sowing, March/May, 1 cm. (½ in.) deep and 8 cm. (3 ins.) apart where to flower. Thin seedlings to 16 cm. (6 ins.) apart.

Under glass: Soak seeds as above. Sow Feb./March in greenhouse/ indoors, singly, 1 cm. (½ in.) deep in 8 cm. (3 ins.) pots of seed compost, or 6 cm. (2½ ins.) apart in seed trays. Provide 13-16°C. Grow in good light, then harden off before planting out 25 cm. (10ins.) apart, April/early May. When there are 3-4 pairs of leaves, pinch out the growing tip. Feed regularly with Sweet Pea fertiliser for best results. Can be sown in pots, Sept./October: wintered in a frame; planted out in April.

Sweet Pea
Jet Set

A very free flowering variety which only grows to about 90 cm. (3 ft.) tall, yet produces long and robust stems of scented blooms in shades of pink, crimson, scarlet, blue and mauve, together with cream. Use in or at the back of beds and borders, or to produce low growing 'hedges' in the garden. Splendid cut flowers, too.

How to grow: Best in rich, well drained soil with a little lime, and in full sun. They are hardy plants sown each year (Hardy Annual).

Outdoors: Soak seeds in water for 12 hours before sowing, March/May, 1 cm. (½ in.) deep and 8 cm. (3 ins.) apart where to flower. Thin seedlings to 16 cm. (6 ins.) apart.

Under glass: Soak seeds as above. Sow Feb./March in greenhouse/ indoors, singly, 1 cm. (½ in.) deep in 8 cm. (3 ins.) pots of seed compost, or 6 cm. (2½ ins.) apart in seed trays. Provide 13-16°C. Grow in good light, then harden off before planting out 22 cm. (9 ins.) apart, April/early May. When there are 3-4 pairs of leaves, pinch out the growing tip. Support the plants with short twiggy sticks, netting or canes and twine. Feed regularly with Sweet Pea fertiliser for best results.

Sweet William
Large Flowered Mixture

Sweet Williams have rounded clusters of flat, open flowers in various shades of pink and red, together with white. They are sweetly scented and appear in June/July on plants growing 45-60 cm. (1½-2 ft.) tall. For beds, borders or as long lasting cut flowers.

How to grow: Sweet Williams will grow in ordinary, well drained soil with a little lime, and in sun. They are hardy plants which you sow one year to flower the next (Hardy Biennial).

Sow thinly, outdoors, in a seed bed of prepared soil during May or June. Cover the seeds lightly with fine soil. When the seedlings are large enough to handle, transplant them 15 cm. (6 ins.) apart. Grow on and by late September/October the plants will be ready to plant, 30-40 cm. (12-15 ins.) apart, in their flowering positions. To do this, lift the plants carefully to avoid root damage and replant into holes, large enough to accommodate the root system, made with a trowel. Firm the soil around the plants.

Tagetes
Golden Gem

A variety with masses of bright, golden coloured flowers carried from July to September on neat, compact plants just 22 cm. (9 ins.) tall. They are ideal for beds or as an edging to borders and beds. Suitable, too, for tubs and window boxes, 'Golden Gem' blends especially well with blue Lobelias.

How to grow: Tagetes will grow in most well cultivated soils, but a moderately fertile soil is best, in a sunny situation. They are fairly hardy plants which you sow each year (Half Hardy Annual).

Outdoors: Sow thinly, late April/May, in prepared moist soil where you want them to flower. Cover seeds lightly. Thin young seedlings to 22 cm. (9 ins.) apart. Surplus seedlings may be transferred elsewhere.

Under glass: Sow thinly, Feb./early April, in a greenhouse/indoors, using seed compost. Cover the seeds lightly with fine compost. Provide 18-21°C. When 2nd set of leaves appears, transfer seedlings 5 cm. (2 ins.) apart into trays of potting compost. Grow in good light, then harden off before planting out, 22 cm. (9 ins.) apart, late May/early June.

Wallflower
Fire King

This orange-red variety is a blaze of colour from April to June. The plants grow 40-45 cm. (15-18 ins.) tall and have stems clustered with strongly scented flowers. For beds and borders — they look lovely with Tulips and Forget-Me-Nots — or as cut flowers.

How to grow: Wallflowers like ordinary, well drained soil with a little lime, and sun. They are hardy plants which you sow one year to flower the next (Hardy Biennial).
Sow thinly, outdoors, in a seed bed of prepared soil during May or June. Cover the seeds lightly with fine soil. When the seedlings are large enough to handle, transplant them 15 cm. (6 ins.) apart. Pinch out the growing tip, when the plants are 12-15 cm. (5-6 ins.) tall, to help them become bushy. By late September/October the plants will be ready to plant, 30 cm. (12 ins.) apart in their flowering positions. To do this, lift the plants carefully to avoid root damage and replant in holes, large enough to accommodate the root system, made with a trowel. Firm the soil around the plants.

Wallflower
Large Flowered Mixture

Bright, showy plants flowering April to June, the stems having clusters of strongly scented blooms in shades of yellow, orange, red, ruby purple and white. They grow 45 cm. (18 ins.) tall and are ideal for massed colour in beds, borders or window boxes. Delightful planted with Tulips and Forget-Me-Nots.

How to grow: Wallflowers like ordinary, well drained soil with a little lime, and sun. They are hardy plants which you sow one year to flower the next (Hardy Biennial).
Sow thinly, outdoors, in a seed bed of prepared soil during May or June. Cover the seeds lightly with fine soil. When the seedlings are large enough to handle, transplant them 15 cm. (6 ins.) apart. Pinch out the growing tip, when the plants are 12-15 cm. (5-6 ins.) tall, to help them become bushy. By late September/October the plants will be ready to plant, 30 cm. (12 ins.) apart in their flowering positions. To do this, lift the plants carefully to avoid root damage and replant in holes, large enough to accommodate the root system, made with a trowel. Firm the soil around the plants.

Siberian Wallflower

The main thing about Siberian Wallflowers is the colour of their flowers — a rich, glowing orange. They bloom from May to July, the scented flowers being produced in clusters on the stems. Of compact habit, the plants reach 30-40 cm. (12-15 ins.) in height and they grow well in beds and borders.

How to grow: Wallflowers like ordinary, well drained soil with a little lime, and sun. They are hardy plants which you sow one year to flower the next (Hardy Biennial).
Sow thinly, outdoors, in a seed bed of prepared soil during May or June. Cover the seeds lightly with fine soil. When the seedlings are large enough to handle, transplant them 15 cm. (6 ins.) apart. Pinch out the growing tip. when the plants are 12-15 cm. (5-6 ins.) tall, to help them become bushy. By late September/October the plants will be ready to plant, 25 cm. (10 ins.) apart in their flowering positions. To do this, lift the plants carefully to avoid root damage and replant in holes, large enough to accommodate the root system, made with a trowel. Firm the soil around the plants.

Zinnia
Mammoth Mixture

A large flowered variety, bushy and 60-75 cm. (2-2½ ft.) tall, with bright coloured blooms in yellow, salmon, pink, scarlet, purple and white from July to October. Zinnias are ideal for beds and borders, and as cut flowers.

How to grow: Zinnias like rich, well drained and cultivated soil in a sunny, sheltered position. They are fairly hardy plants which you sow each year (Half Hardy Annual).

Outdoors: Sow thinly, during May, in prepared moist soil where they are to flower. Cover the seeds lightly with fine soil. Thin young seedlings to 30 cm. (12 ins.) apart. Surplus seedlings may be transferred elsewhere, avoiding root disturbance as far as possible.

Under glass: sow thinly, March/April, in a greenhouse/indoors, using seed compost. Cover the seeds lightly. Provide 20-24°C. When 2nd set of leaves appears, transfer seedlings to individual 8 cm. (3 ins.) pots of compost. Grow in good light, then harden off before planting out, late May/early June. Pinch out growing tip when 12 cm (5 ins.) tall. Remove dead blooms to prolong the flowering display.

Zinnia
Thumbelina

A dwarf, compact variety with double and semi-double flowers about 4 cm. (1½ ins.) across in a wide range of bright colours, from July to September. The plants grow 15 cm. (6 ins.) tall making them an excellent choice for the front of beds and borders, or in tubs and window boxes.

How to grow: Zinnias like rich, well drained and cultivated soil in a sunny, sheltered position. They are fairly hardy plants which you sow each year (Half Hardy Annual).

Outdoors: Sow thinly, during May, in prepared moist soil where they are to flower. Cover the seeds lightly with fine soil. Thin young seedlings to 15 cm. (6 ins.) apart. Surplus seedlings may be transferred elsewhere, avoiding root disturbance as far as possible.

Under glass: Sow thinly, March/April, in a greenhouse/indoors, using seed compost. Cover the seeds lightly. Provide 20-24°C. When 2nd set of leaves appears, transfer seedlings to individual 8 cm. (3 ins.) pots of compost. Grow in good light, then harden off before planting out, late May/early June. Remove dead blooms to prolong the flowering display.

VEGETABLES FROM SEED

Leaf Beet
Perpetual Spinach

An excellent vegetable with succulent leaves which are cooked like spinach. Valuable under dry conditions where true spinach runs to seed and, because of its hardiness, very useful for harvesting in autumn and winter. Leaf Beet will tolerate light shade.

How to grow: Best grown in fertile, well drained, but moisture-retentive soil with plenty of rotted manure or garden compost added.
Sow outdoors, April/May, for harvesting from the end of May/early June through the summer and winter (possibly into following spring). Sow again in July crops in autumn/winter through to the summer. Set 3-4 seeds, 1-2 cm. (½-¾ in.) deep, 22 cm. (9 ins.) apart in rows 40 cm. (15 ins.) apart. When 2nd set of leaves appears, thin seedlings to leave one at each position. Pick young, tender leaves, as near to the ground as possible, taking a few of the largest leaves from each plant at regular intervals. Alternatively, cut a whole plant about 3 cm. (1 in.) above soil level and leave it to re-sprout. In dry weather keep the plants watered. Remove any flower heads. Cover overwintered plants with cloches for best results.

Beetroot
Boltardy

Resistant to bolting (running to seed) and, thus, can be sown early. Globe shaped roots with smooth skin and deep red flesh which is firm and succulent. May be grated and eaten raw, boiled and served cold with salads, freshly boiled and eaten hot with butter, or pickled.

How to grow: Beetroot grows best in well drained, fertile soil which has been manured for a different crop in the previous growing season. Avoid freshly manured soil.
Soak the seeds in tepid water for ½-1 hour before sowing: do not sow when soil temperature is below 7°C. For an early crop, sow late February/early March under cloches/in a frame, or outdoors late March/early April. Set seeds, in moist soil, 1-2 cm. (½-¾ in.) deep and 10 cm. (4 ins.) apart with rows 18 cm. (7 ins.) apart. For maincrops and winter storage, make several sowings from April to early July, 3 cm. (1 in.) apart in rows 30 cm. (1 ft.) apart. When 2nd set of leaves appears, thin seedlings to one at each position. For winter use, lift carefully in October, twist off leaves just above the root: store in boxes of damp sand in a cool frost-free place.

Beetroot
Crimson Globe

A favourite globe shaped variety with deep red flesh of fine flavour and quality. Beetroot may be grated and eaten raw, boiled and served cold with salads, freshly boiled and eaten hot with butter, or pickled.

How to grow: Beetroot grows best in well drained fertile soil which has been manured for a different crop in the previous growing season. Avoid freshly manured soil.

To assist germination, soak the seeds in tepid water for ½-1 hour before sowing. Do not sow too early or when soil temperature is below 7°C. For maincrops and winter storage, make several sowings from May to early July, setting seeds, in moist soil, 1-2 cm. (½-¾ in.) deep and 3 cm. (1 in.) apart in rows 30 cm. (1 ft.) apart. When 2nd set of leaves appears, thin seedlings to one at each position. Harvest when the roots are large enough. For winter use, lift carefully in October, twist off leaves just above the root: store in boxes of damp sand in a cool, frost-free place. May also be stored cool (near freezing point) in polythene bags with bag folded over to restrict ventilation.

Sprouting Broccoli
Early Purple Sprouting

A most useful vegetable which is very hardy and is ready to harvest from February through to May. Produces an abundant supply of purple heads on short stalks. Suitable for freezing.

How to grow: Best in reasonably fertile, firm, moist soil with a little lime, in a sunny position. You sow one year to have them ready to use the next. Sow thinly, 2-2½ cm. (¾-1 in.) deep, in a seed bed of prepared soil, mid April/mid May. Thin seedlings to 3-5 cm. (1-2 ins.) apart once they can be handled and, in June/July, when about 10 cm. (4 ins.) tall, transplant them to the cropping positions at 70 cm. (27 ins.) apart each way (75 cm./30 ins. on rich soils). Plant firmly into firm ground. Water in well. When the plants are well developed, draw a little soil around the base of the stems for support. Water during dry weather. The heads or 'spears' are ready to harvest when well formed but before the flowers have begun to open. Cut or snap the central spear first, when about 10 cm. (4 ins.) long, and then harvest the side shoots at regular intervals.

Sprouting Broccoli
Green Sprouting

Calabrese is quick growing with a delicious flavour. It crops August/October, producing a central green flowerhead followed by smaller heads or 'spears'. Cook and serve with butter. Suitable for freezing.

How to grow: Best in reasonably fertile, firm, moist soil with a little lime, in a sunny position.
Sow, where the plants are to mature, in cultivated but firm, moist soil, April/May with a successional sowing in June. Set several seeds, 2-2½ cm. (¾-1 in.) deep, at 15 cm. (6 ins.) intervals in rows 30 cm. (1 ft.) apart. When the 2nd set of leaves appears, thin to one seedling at each position. It is important to keep the plants well watered during dry weather. Cut the central head first. This stimulates the development of the side shoots which can be further assisted by applying a light dressing of a general fertiliser at this time. Harvest the spears regularly when they are about 10 cm. (4 ins.) long.

Brussels Sprouts
Groninger — Stiekema

A popular winter vegetable producing large quantities of firm sprouts from November through the winter. When all the sprouts have been harvested, the tufts of leaves at the top are also good to eat as 'winter greens'.

How to grow: Best in good, fertile soil with a little lime, in an open position sheltered from strong winds. Full sun is preferable though sprouts will tolerate light shade.
Sow thinly, 2-2½ cm. (¾-1 in.) deep, in a seed bed of prepared soil, mid March/late April. Thin seedlings to 3-5 cm. (1-2 ins.) apart once they can be handled and, mid May/June, when about 10 cm. (4 ins.) tall, transfer to the cropping positions at 90 cm. (3 ft.) apart each way. Plant firmly into firm ground. Set the plants with lowest leaf at soil level and water them in well. Draw a little soil around the base of the stems about a month after planting, for support. Harvest from the bottom of the plants, working upwards as sprouts mature. Snap off the sprouts, using your fingers, with a downward movement. Sprouts taste better after the first frosts.

Cabbage
Golden Acre

Produces round heads and firm, solid hearts with few outer leaves. Quick growing and ready to cut in June, continuing to September with successional sowings.

How to grow: Best in fertile, firm, moist soil with a little lime, in an open position.

Under glass: For early summer cabbage, sow thinly, in a greenhouse/indoors at 13°C late Feb./early March, in seed compost. When 2nd set of leaves appears, transfer seedlings 5 cm. (2 ins.) apart into trays of potting compost. Grow in good light, then harden off — for example, in a cold frame — before planting out in April, 35 cm. (14 ins.) apart each way for small heads — or at 45 cm. (18 ins.) for larger heads. Plant firmly into firm ground: water in well.

Outdoors: Sow thinly, 2-2½ cm. (¾-1 in.) deep, in a seed bed of prepared soil, mid March/May, making several sowings for succession. Thin seedlings to 3-5 cm. (1-2 ins.) apart once they can be handled and then, late April/June, when about 10 cm. (4 ins.) tall, transplant them to their cropping positions. When well established, apply a dressing of general fertiliser.

Cabbage
Greyhound

Compact growing, having solid, pointed heads of fine quality with few outer leaves. Quick maturing and ready to cut in June, continuing to September with successional sowings.

How to grow: Best in fertile, firm, moist soil with a little lime, in an open position.

Under glass: For early summer cabbage, sow thinly, in a greenhouse/indoors at 13°C late Feb./early March, in seed compost. When 2nd set of leaves appears, transfer seedlings 5 cm. (2 ins.) apart into trays of potting compost. Grow in good light, then harden off — for example, in a cold frame — before planting out in April, 35 cm. (14 ins.) apart each way for small heads — or at 45 cm. (18 ins.) for larger heads. Plant firmly into firm ground: water in well.

Outdoors: Sow thinly, 2-2½ cm. (¾-1 in.) deep, in a seed bed of prepared soil, mid March/May, making several sowings for succession. Thin seedlings to 3-5 cm. (1-2 ins.) apart once they can be handled and then, late April/June, when about 10 cm. (4 ins.) tall, transplant them to their cropping positions. When well established, apply a general fertiliser.

Cabbage
Offenham - Flower of Spring

A hardy variety producing large, pointed hearts of good flavour during April and May. Can also be grown to produce 'spring greens'.

How to grow: Best in well drained, fertile, firm soil with a little lime, in an open, sunny position. You sow one year to have them ready to use the next.

Sow thinly, 2-2½ cm. (¾-1 in.) deep, in a seed bed, late July in the north/ cold areas; early August in the south.

Thin seedlings to 3-5 cm. (1-2 ins.) apart once they can be handled and, mid September/early October, transplant to cropping positions at 30 cm. (12 ins.) apart each way. Plant firmly into firm ground: water in well. For 'spring greens', plant in rows 30 cm. (12 ins.) apart with 10 cm. (4 ins.) between plants. Leave them to produce 'greens' or, in early spring, take 2 out of every 3 plants in the row for 'greens' leaving remaining plants at 30 x 30 cm. (12 x 12 ins.) to heart up. 2 weeks after planting out, draw a little soil around base of the plants. Firm any plants loosened by adverse winter weather. In early March, apply sulphate of ammonia fertiliser at 70 g. per sq. metre (2 oz. per sq. yd.) to encourage hearting.

Cabbage
Primo

An early variety with round heads and firm, solid hearts which are good for salads as well as cooking. They grow quickly and are ready to cut in June, continuing to September with successional sowings.

How to grow: Best in fertile, firm, moist soil with a little lime, in an open position.

Under glass: For early summer cabbage, sow thinly, in a greenhouse/indoors at 13°C late Feb./ early March, in seed compost. When 2nd set of leaves appears, transfer seedlings 5 cm. (2 ins.) apart into trays of potting compost. Grow in good light, then harden off — for example, in a cold frame — before planting out in April, 35 cm. (14 ins.) apart each way for small heads — or at 45 cm. (18 ins.) for larger heads. Plant firmly into firm ground: water in well.

Outdoors: Sow thinly, 2-2½ cm. (¾-1 in.) deep, in a seed bed of prepared soil, mid March/May, making several sowings for succession. Thin seedlings to 3-5 cm. (1-2 ins.) apart once they can be handled and then, late April/June, when about 10 cm. (4 ins.) tall, transplant them to their cropping positions. When well established, apply a general fertiliser.

Savoy Cabbage
Best of All

A winter cabbage ready for cutting from October to December. It is a hardy variety with large, solid hearts and crinkly leaves. Easy to grow and very tasty.

How to grow: These cabbages grow best in well drained but moist, fertile, firm soil with a little lime, in an open position.
Set seeds thinly, 2-2½ cm. (¾-1 in.) deep, in a seed bed of prepared soil, late April/May, making several sowings for succession. Thin the seedlings to 3-5 cm. (1-2 ins.) apart once they can be handled and, in June/July, when they are about 10 cm. (4 ins.) tall, transplant them to their cropping positions in rows spaced 45 cm. (18 ins.) apart, leaving 45 cm. (18 ins.) between plants. It is important to plant firmly into firm ground. Water in the plants well. Harvest Savoy cabbages when they have formed a good heart.

Carrot
Autumn King

A large, tapering, blunt-ended variety which produces a big crop of fine flavoured carrots. Recommended to use fresh during late summer/autumn, and for winter storage.

How to grow: These carrots grow best in deep, rich, well drained soil that is stone-free and of light or medium texture. Avoid freshly manured soil. Choose an open position.
Sow very thinly, 1-2 cm. (½-¾ in.) deep in rows 15 cm. (6 ins.) apart, April/late May, outdoors. When 2nd set of leaves appears, thin the seedlings to 4 cm. (1½ ins.) apart for medium size carrots: allow 15 cm. (6 ins.) for larger carrots. To help prevent carrot fly, thin in the evening on a dull day, firm the soil around remaining plants and water them. Bury thinnings in the compost heap. For winter use, lift as required, from light, well drained soils. For protection before harvesting, cut off tops in early December, scatter slug pellets, then cover with a 30 cm. (1 ft.) layer of leaves/straw. Or lift in October, remove soil, cut off tops 1 cm. (½ in.) above crown: store in boxes of damp sand in a cool, frost-free place.

Carrot
Chantenay Red Cored

Early maincrop variety with medium size conical roots of rich colour and fine flavour with very little core. For summer and autumn harvest. Suitable, too, for freezing.

How to grow: These carrots grow best in fairly deep, rich, well drained soil that is stone-free and of light or medium texture. Avoid freshly manured soil. Choose an open position. Set seeds very thinly, 1-2 cm. (½-¾ in.) deep in rows 15 cm. (6 ins.) apart, April to June, outdoors where the plants are to mature. Make several sowings for succession. When the 2nd set of leaves appears, thin the seedlings to 4 cm. (1½ ins.) apart. To help prevent carrot fly, thin in the evening on a dull day, firm the soil around remaining plants and water them. Bury thinnings in the compost heap. Harvest from August to November. This variety may be stored for winter, though 'Autumn King' is particularly recommended for this purpose. To store, lift in October, remove soil, cut off tops 1 cm. (½ in.) above crown, and store in boxes of damp sand in a cool, frost-free place.

Carrot
Early Nantes

If you enjoy the taste of young carrots, fresh from the garden, this early variety is ideal. The carrots are small and tender with a sweet flavour. Ready for use from mid May through to October from successional sowings. Suitable, too, for freezing.

How to grow: These carrots grow best in fairly deep, rich, well drained soil that is stone-free and of light or medium texture. Avoid freshly manured soil. Choose an open position.
Sow January to March in cold frames/under cloches; or outdoors, every 3-4 weeks, March to mid July. Do not sow when the soil temperature is below 7°C. Set seeds very thinly, 1-2 cm. (½-¾ in.) deep in rows 15 cm. (6 ins.) apart. When the 2nd set of leaves appears, thin the seedlings to 10 cm. (4 ins.) apart for early crops: to 4 cm. (1½ ins.) apart for later crops. To help prevent carrot fly, thin in the evening on a dull day, firm the soil around remaining plants and water them. Bury thinnings in the compost heap.

Carrot
Kundulus

An early maincrop variety which is very good for shallow soils. It produces round-shouldered, globe-shaped roots about 4 cm. (1½ ins.) across and 7 cm. (2¾ ins.) long when mature. They are of good colour right through and resistant to splitting. May be pulled and eaten young, being ideal at this stage for grating raw into salads.

How to grow: These carrots grow best in rich, well drained soil that is stone-free and of light or medium texture. Avoid freshly manured soil. Choose an open position. Set seeds very thinly, 1-2 cm. (½-¾ in.) deep in rows 15 cm. (6 ins.) apart, April to mid July, outdoors where the plants are to mature. Make several sowings for succession. When the 2nd set of leaves appears, thin the seedlings to 4 cm. (1½ ins.) apart. To help prevent carrot fly, thin in the evening on a dull day, firm the soil around remaining plants and water them. Bury thinnings in the compost heap. Harvest from early July to October.

Cauliflower Snowball

Compact and early maturing with pure white heads of good quality and fine flavour. Ready from June to September with successional sowings. Suitable, too, for freezing.

How to grow: Best in deeply dug, fertile, firm soil which is moisture-retentive and has a little lime. Choose a sunny position.

Under glass: Sow January at 13°C in a greenhouse/indoors. When 2nd set of leaves appears, transfer seedlings, 1 to an 8-9 cm. (3-3½ ins.) pot. Grow on in good light, then harden off before planting out March/early April, firmly into firm ground at 53 cm. (21 ins.) apart each way. Sow March to plant mid May. Can be sown 1st week Oct., transferred to pots in cold frame, to plant out in March.

Outdoors: Sow thinly, 2-2½ cm. (¾-1 in.) deep in a seed bed, late April/early May. Thin seedlings to 3-5 cm. (1-2 ins.) apart: transfer to cropping positions, mid June, at 70 cm. (27 ins.) apart each way. Plant firmly. Harvest late August/September. Water well in dry weather. Protect nearly mature heads from sun by snapping 1-2 large leaves and bending them over the curds.

Cauliflower English Winter
Snow's Winter White

This variety grows through the winter and the pure white heads are ready for harvesting in February/March, or a little earlier.

How to grow: Best in deeply dug, reasonably fertile, firm soil with a little lime. It should be moisture-retentive but well drained. Choose a sunny, sheltered position. You sow one year to have them ready to use the next. Sow thinly, 2-2½ cm. (¾-1 in.) deep in a seed bed of prepared soil, late March/April. Thin seedlings to 3-5 cm. (1-2 ins.) apart once they can be handled and, in May/June, when they are about 6 weeks old, transplant them to their cropping positions at 75 cm. (30 ins.) apart each way. Plant firmly into firm ground. Keep the plants well watered during dry weather. As the heads begin to swell, snap 1-2 leaves and bend them over the curds to protect them from hard weather.

Celery
Golden Self Blanching

This variety produces compact heads with crisp, yellow stems of good quality and fine, nutty flavour. Earthing up is not required. Ready for use August to October.

How to grow: Celery needs a rich, well drained but moisture-retentive soil, with a little lime, in an open position. Dig in plenty of rotted manure or garden compost.
Sow thinly, at 13-16°C from the 3rd week of March to early April. Set the seeds on the compost surface and press them in lightly. Do not exclude light. When the 2nd set of leaves appears, transfer the seedlings to individual 8 cm. (3 ins.) pots, or 6 cm. (2½ ins.) apart in trays of potting compost. Grow in good light with a minimum of 10°C then harden off before planting out in late May/early June when no frost danger. Set in blocks, with 28 cm. (11 ins.) each way between plants or, for slender hearts, at 15 cm. (6 ins.) apart. Keep plants well watered during dry weather. When well established, tuck straw around plants on the outside of the block to assist blanching. Complete all harvesting before sharp frosts.

Chives

A herb, 20-25 cm. (8-10 ins.) tall, with a delicate onion-like flavour and decorative mauve flowers. Easy to grow in window boxes/pots as well as in the garden. Use the leaves, from early May to October, in salads, sandwiches, soups, and cheese or egg dishes.

How to grow: Grows best in fertile, well drained soil with a little lime. It should be moisture-retentive but well drained. Choose a sunny position or one in light, partial shade.
Sow thinly, 1 cm. (¹/₂ in.) deep, in prepared soil, mid March/July. Thin or transplant the young seedlings to 22 cm. (9 ins.) apart each way. In dry weather, water frequently. Allow plants to become well established before cropping for the first time. Harvest by cutting the leaves close to the ground, but do not cut all the leaves from a plant at one time. Regular cutting encourages further growth. Remove faded flower heads. For winter use, especially, Chives can be grown in 12 cm. (5 ins.) pots in a warm, light place indoors. Outdoors, Chives die down in winter but they will grow again the next spring. Apply some general fertiliser in March.

Cress Fine Curled

Cress is usually grown and used with mustard as a garnish and to flavour salads and sandwiches. It has an appetising taste, a little milder than mustard. Curled cress has bright green wavy leaves on white stems. It is most useful because it can be grown very easily all year round.

How to grow: Sow cress whenever you want and it will be ready to cut in about 14 days. Sow the seeds at a minimum temperature of 10°C, fairly thickly, in shallow trays or punnets filled with moist seed compost. Press the seeds into the surface and cover the tray with brown paper or black polythene for a few days until the seeds have germinated. Then move the tray onto the kitchen windowsill. Can also be sown on a layer of moistened kitchen tissue in the bottom of a shallow dish. Keep the tissue watered and cover, initially, as for growing in compost. When 5 cm. (2 ins.) tall, cut the cress at the base of the stems using a pair of scissors. To have mustard and cress ready at the same time, sow cress three days before the mustard.

Cucumber
Delicatesse

An easy to grow variety for outdoor cultivation. Produces a good crop of crisp, well flavoured cucumbers — shorter and fatter than greenhouse sorts — from July to September.

How to grow: Likes very fertile, moisture-retentive soil in a sheltered, sunny position. Best to prepare individual sowing/planting positions about 30 cm. (12 ins.) deep and 45 cm. (18 ins.) wide adding plenty of well rotted manure/garden compost, with the top 15-20 cm. (6-8 ins.) manure-free and slightly mounded above surrounding soil. Plants should be 60-75 cm. (2-2½ ft.) apart.

Under glass: Sow mid April/early May at 21°C, 2 cm. (¾ in.) deep, singly in 8 cm. (3 ins.) pots. Harden off before planting out, end May/early June when no frost risk.

Outdoors: Sow mid May (south); end May/early June (north), 2 cm. (¾ in.) deep, setting 2-3 seeds per mound. Cover with jam jars/cloches until germination. When 2nd set of leaves has developed, thin plants to one at each position. Pinch out growing tips at the 5-6 leaf stage. Spread out resulting side shoots. Retain male and female flowers. Keep well watered and feed regularly.

Cucumber
Telegraph

A greenhouse variety producing an excellent crop of smooth-skinned, good-sized fruits that are crisp and of fine flavour. Harvest from May to September.

How to grow: Set seeds 2 cm. (¾ in.) deep, singly in 8 cm. (3 ins.) pots of seed compost, at 21°C. Sow late February/late April bearing in mind that a minimum of 18°C is required as plants develop. Plant late March onwards (late May if greenhouse unheated), at about the 4-leaf stage, when the pots are filled with roots. Grow 60 cm. (2 ft.) apart in a well prepared bed containing plenty of well rotted manure/garden compost. May also be planted in growing bags or grow one to a 25 cm. (10 ins.) pot. Maintain warmth and humidity. Keep the plants well watered and feed regularly. Tie stems to horizontal wires set about 22 cm. (9 ins.) apart, or to long, upright canes, or twist them round vertical strings. Pinch out the growing point when plants reach the roof. Remove tendrils and male flowers (those without a tiny 'embryo' cucumber behind the petals). Pinch out side shoots at the 2nd leaf and the sub-laterals, which develop from them, at the 1st leaf. Provide light shade from strong summer sun.

Leek
Autumn Mammoth - Argenta

Delicious and mildly flavoured with good quality stems of tender, white flesh. Ready October to December — or later if weather remains open.

How to grow: Best in rich, deeply dug, well drained soil with plenty of rotted manure/garden compost. Choose an open position.

Outdoors: Sow thinly, 1-2 cm. (½-¾ in.) deep in a seed bed, mid March/April. In early May, thin seedlings to 1-2½ cm. (½-1 in.) apart: firm around those remaining. Move to cropping positions, late May/June, when 15-20 cm. (6-8 ins.) tall. Plant in rows 30 cm. (12 ins.) apart with 15 cm. (6 ins.) between plants. Make 5 cm. (2 ins.) wide holes, 15 cm. (6 ins.) deep, with a dibber and drop 1 plant in each. Fill hole with water to settle the soil around the roots. For the longest possible white stems, gradually draw up soil around the plants as they develop.

Under glass: For earlier, larger leeks, sow thinly in a greenhouse/indoors at 13°C, in February. When large enough to handle, transfer seedlings 5 cm. (2 ins.) apart into trays of potting compost. Grow in good light, then harden off before planting out in May.

Leek
Musselburgh

Very hardy, with long, thick, white stems of excellent quality which have a delicate onion flavour. Harvest November to March/April.

How to grow: Best in rich, deeply dug, well drained soil with plenty of rotted manure/garden compost. Choose an open postion.

Outdoors: Sow thinly, 1-2 cm. (½-¾ in.) deep in a seed bed, mid March/April. In early May, thin seedlings to 1-2½ cm. (½-1 in.) apart: firm around those remaining. Move to cropping positions, late May/June, when 15-20 cm. (6-8 ins.) tall. Plant in rows 30 cm. (12 ins.) apart with 15 cm. (6 ins.) between plants. Make 5 cm. (2 ins.) wide holes, 15 cm. (6 ins.) deep, with a dibber and drop 1 plant in each. Fill hole with water to settle the soil around the roots. For the longest possible white stems, gradually draw up soil around the plants as they develop.

Under glass: For earlier, larger leeks, sow thinly in a greenhouse/indoors at 13°C, in February. When large enough to handle, transfer seedlings 5 cm. (2 ins.) apart into trays of potting compost. Grow in good light, then harden off before planting out in May.

Lettuce
All the Year Round

A compact growing, reliable butterhead variety which has crisp, white hearts. Can be sown to produce spring, summer and autumn crops.

How to grow: Best in fairly rich, moist, but well drained soil in an open position.

Under glass: Sow thinly in cold frame/under cloches, mid Feb. (in south); early March (north). Thin the young seedlings to 22 cm. (9 ins.) apart each way. Can be sown in trays in a greenhouse to plant out under cloches or outdoors where sheltered, end March/early April. Harvest late May/June.

Outdoors: Sow thinly, in moist soil where the plants are to mature, 1 cm. (½ in.) deep in rows 30 cm. (1 ft.) apart. Thin the young seedlings 30 cm. (12 ins.) apart. Except in mid summer, thinnings may be transplanted elsewhere. Sow fortnightly, late March-early August for June-October harvest. Water well in dry weather. For spring crops, sow thinly, late Aug./early Sept. in rows 25 cm. (10 ins.) apart. In mid/late Sept. thin to 5-8 cm. (2-3 ins.) apart. Thin to 30 cm. (12 ins.) apart in early March; apply some general fertiliser. Harvest in May. Can be covered with cloches in winter.

Cos Lettuce
Paris White

An upright growing, oval-shaped lettuce with very crisp, tender leaves of fine flavour. Harvest, when the hearts are fully formed, June to September, or grow as 'Leaf Lettuce'

How to grow: Best in rich, moisture-retentive but well drained soil in an open position.

Sow very thinly, where the plants are to mature, 1 cm. (½ in.) deep, in rows 30 cm. (1 ft.) apart. When the 2nd set of leaves appears, thin the seedlings to 30 cm. (1 ft.) apart. Except in mid summer, thinnings may be transplanted elsewhere: avoid root disturbance as far as possible. Sow at about 2 week intervals, late March to late July. Water well during dry weather. This variety does not need tying to produce a compact heart.

Leaf Lettuce: For leafy, non-hearting lettuce, sow in rows 12 cm. (5 ins.) apart, aiming to have 12-15 plants per 30 cm. (1 ft.) of row. Harvest 40-50 days after sowing, cutting leaves 3 cm. (1 in.) above soil level. Leave the stump to produce a further crop 5-7 weeks later. For continuous supplies mid May-mid October, sow weekly early April-mid May, plus weekly sowings in first 3 weeks of August.

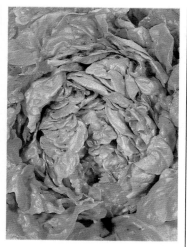

Lettuce
Salad Bowl

Produces deliciously flavoured, curled and fringed leaves in abundance. An especially useful variety since the leaves are picked as required, without cutting the whole plant. Slow to run to seed even in hot, dry weather. Harvest late May to October.

How to grow: Best in fairly rich, moist, but well drained soil in an open position.

Under glass: Sow thinly in cold frame/under cloches, mid February (in south); early March (north). Thin seedlings, once they can be handled, to 22 cm. (9 ins.) apart each way. Can be sown in trays in a greenhouse to plant out under cloches or outdoors where sheltered, end March/early April. Harvest late May/June.

Outdoors: Sow thinly, in moist soil where the plants are to mature, 1 cm. (½ in.) deep in rows 30 cm. (1 ft.) apart. Thin the young seedlings 30 cm. (12 ins.) apart. Except in mid summer, thinnings may be transplanted elsewhere. Make successional sowings, late March-early August for June-October harvest. Water well in dry weather. Pick the leaves as required, taking a few of the outermost leaves at each harvest.

Lettuce
Tom Thumb

This variety is compact growing with small, solid heads and few outer leaves. Very crisp and sweet. Harvest from late May to October.

How to grow: Best in fairly rich, moisture-retentive but well drained soil in an open position.

Under glass: Sow thinly in a cold frame or under cloches, mid February (in south); early March (north). Thin the seedlings, once they can be handled, to 20 cm. (8 ins.) apart each way. Can be sown in trays in a greenhouse to plant out under cloches or outdoors where sheltered, end March/early April. Harvest late May/June.

Outdoors: Sow very thinly, in moist soil where the plants are to mature, 1 cm. (½ in.) deep in rows 22 cm. (9 ins.) apart. When the 2nd set of leaves appears, thin the seedlings to 22 cm. (9 ins.) apart. Except in mid-summer, thinnings may be transplanted elsewhere, avoiding root disturbance as far as possible. Sow at about 2 week intervals, late March to early August for harvest June to October. Water well in dry weather.

Lettuce
Valdor

A hardy, spring maturing variety, for autumn sowing, with large heads and deep green, solid hearts.

How to grow: Best in fertile, moist but well drained soil in an open but sheltered position.

Sow thinly, late August/early September, in moist soil where the plants are to mature, 1 cm. (1/2 in.) deep in rows 25 cm. (10 ins.) apart. In mid/late September when the seedlings are 1 cm. (1/2 in.) tall, thin them to 5-8 cm. (2-3 ins.) apart. During early March, make a further thinning to leave the plants about 30 cm. (12 ins.) apart in the rows. Then apply a dressing of general fertiliser. If the weather is dry, water the plants in late April/May. Harvest the crop during May and early June. During hard winter weather, the plants can be covered with cloches.

Lettuce
Webbs Wonderful

A large variety, producing firm, crinkly leaves which curl inwards to form tightly packed hearts that are crisp and well flavoured. Slow to run to seed. Harvest June to October.

How to grow: Best in fairly rich, moisture-retentive but well drained soil in an open position.

Sow very thinly, where the plants are to mature, 1 cm. (1/2 in.) deep, in rows 30 cm. (1 ft.) apart. When the 2nd set of leaves appears, thin the seedlings to 40 cm. (15 ins.) apart. Except in mid summer, thinnings may be transplanted elsewhere, avoiding root disturbances as far as possible. Sow at about 2 week intervals, late March to late July. Water well during dry weather. During summer, avoid very high soil temperatures as germination can be adversely affected. To assist, water seed row before sowing and shade the soil beforehand if necessary.

Marrow
F¹ Zucchini

Produces an excellent crop of tasty courgettes — small, immature marrows — that are harvested, when 10-15 cm. (4-6 ins.) long, from July to September. Use fresh or freeze.

How to grow: Likes rich, moist but well drained soil in a warm, sunny position. Prepare individual sowing/ planting positions about 30 cm. (12 ins.) deep, 45 cm. (18 ins.) wide adding plenty of rotted manure/ garden compost, with top 15-20 cm. (6-8 ins.) manure-free and slightly mounded above surrounding soil. Plants should be 90 cm. (3 ft.) apart.

Under glass: Sow mid/late April at 18°C, 2 cm. (¾ in.) deep, singly in 8 cm. (3 ins.) pots. Harden off before planting out at end May/early June, when no frost risk.

Outdoors: Sow mid May/early June, 2 cm. (¾ in.) deep, setting 2-3 seeds per mound. Cover with jam jars/ cloches until germination. At 3-4 leaf stage, thin plants to 1 at each position. Water well and feed regularly; harvest frequently. Male and female flowers are produced and needed for fruit setting. Early in season or during cold weather, take pollen-bearing male flowers and push them into centre of female flowers.

Marrow
Green Bush

Compact growing, with an abundant crop of striped green fruits. Harvest when about 20 cm. (8 ins.) long, from August to October. A plant can produce about 20 marrows.

How to grow: Likes rich, moist but well drained soil in a warm, sunny position. Prepare individual sowing/ planting positions about 30 cm. (12 ins.) deep, 45 cm. (18 ins.) wide adding plenty of rotted manure/ garden compost, with top 15-20 cm. (6-8 ins.) manure-free and slightly mounded above surrounding soil. Plants should be 90 cm. (3 ft.) apart.

Under glass: Sow mid/late April at 18°C, 2 cm. (¾ in.) deep, singly in 8 cm. (3 ins.) pots. Harden off before planting out end May/early June, when no frost risk.

Outdoors: Sow mid May/early June, 2 cm. (¾ in.) deep, setting 2-3 seeds per mound. Cover with jam jars/ cloches until germination. At 3-4 leaf stage, thin plants to 1 at each position. Water well and feed regularly. Male and female flowers are produced and needed for fruit setting. Early in season or during cold weather, take pollen-bearing male flowers and push them into centre of female flowers (those with a tiny 'embryo' fruit behind the petals).

Mustard
White

Mustard has a tangy, pungent taste. It is usually grown and used with cress as a garnish and to flavour salads and sandwiches. Mustard is most useful because it can be grown very easily all year round.

How to grow: Sow mustard whenever you want and it will be ready to cut in about 11 days. Sow the seeds at a minimum temperature of 10°C, fairly thickly, in shallow trays or punnets filled with moist seed compost. Press the seeds into the surface and cover the tray with brown paper or black polythene for a few days until the seeds have germinated. Then move the tray onto the kitchen windowsill.

Can also be sown on a layer of moistened kitchen tissue in the bottom of a shallow dish. Keep the tissue watered and cover, initially, as for growing in compost. When 5 cm. (2 ins.) tall, cut the mustard at the base of the stems using a pair of scissors. To have mustard and cress ready at the same time, sow cress three days before the mustard.

Onion
Ailsa Craig

Large, globe-shaped onions of fine quality and mild flavour. Excellent for exhibition. Ready late August/mid September (July/August is sown previous August). Stores well.

How to grow: Fertile. moist. well drained soil. with little lime, in a sunny position. Avoid freshly manured soil.

Under glass: Sow thinly, in a greenhouse at 16°C, Jan./Feb. When 4 cm. (1½ ins.) tall, transfer seedlings 5-8 cm. (2-3 ins.) apart into trays of potting compost. Grow on, then harden off before planting out, early/mid April, in rows 30 cm. (1 ft.) apart with 4 cm. (1½ ins.) between plants (8-10 cm./3-4 ins. for large onions).

Outdoors: Sow in prepared soil (at minimum of 7°C), March/early April. Set seeds thinly, 1-2 cm. (½-¾ in.) deep in rows 30 cm. (1 ft.) apart. Once seedlings have straightened up, thin them to 4 cm. (1½ ins.) apart (more for large onions). To store, harvest late Aug./mid Sept. when leaves have toppled and started to die back. Lay out the onions to dry for a week or so. Store in a cool, dry, airy place in slatted trays, nets, or made into 'ropes' to hang up. For July/August harvest, sow August, with seeds 2½ cm. (1 in.) apart in rows. Thin to 5 cm. (2 ins.) apart March/April.

Onion
The Queen

This is the variety to grow for pickling, the plants producing small, silver-skinned onions of excellent quality and fine flavour. May be pickled raw or cooked, and the onions can be included with cauliflower and gherkins as mixed pickles.

How to grow: Best grown in reasonably fertile, moist but well drained soil, with a little lime, in a sunny position.
Sow the seeds during March and April where the plants are to mature. Set the seeds 1-2 cm. (½-¾ in.) deep and about ½ cm. (¼ in.) apart with 30 cm. (1 ft.) between rows. May also be sown in bands about 22 cm. (9 ins.) wide, setting the seeds ½ cm. (¼ in.) apart. Do not thin the seedlings. Harvest the onions in July/August and dry them off. For raw pickling, steep the unpeeled onions in brine for 12 hours, then peel them and cover with fresh brine for 24 hours. Rinse and drain well. Pack into clean jars and cover with spiced or white wine vinegar. Store for 3 months before eating. Prepare brine using 500 g. of block salt to 5 litres of water (1 lb. to 1 gallon).

Onion
White Lisbon

This is an excellent variety to produce 'spring onions' for salads. They are tasty, but not too sharp, and have a clear white skin. Can be sown to provide crops from April through to the autumn.

How to grow: Best grown in reasonably fertile, moist but well drained soil, with a little lime, in a sunny position.
Set the seeds reasonably thinly, 1-2 cm. (½-¾ in.) deep, in rows 10 cm. (4 ins.) apart, aiming for plants 2½ cm. (1 in.) apart in the rows. Alternatively, sow in an 8 cm. (3 ins.) wide band with 30 cm. (1 ft.) between the centres of adjacent bands. Sow (with a minimum soil temperature of 7°C) at about 2 week intervals from late February/early March (under cloches) to mid June for crops from June onwards. For harvesting April to June, sow mid August to early September. Earlier crops may be had by protecting the plants with cloches throughout, or for the latter part of the winter. Harvest before the bases of the onions swell.

Parsley
Moss Curled

A mildly spicy herb, rich in vitamins, for garnishing and cooking. Use in stocks, soups and stews and with fish or vegetable dishes.

How to grow: Best in fertile, moist but well drained soil, in a sunny or partially shaded position.

Under glass: Sow thinly in February/March at 16°C in a greenhouse/indoors. When 2nd set of leaves appears, transfer seedlings 5 cm. (2 ins.) apart into trays of potting compost. Grow on in good light, then harden off before planting out in April/May, 15 cm. (6 ins.) apart each way.

Outdoor: Sow thinly, 1-2 cm. ($\frac{1}{2}$-$\frac{3}{4}$ in.) deep, in row 15 cm. (5 ins.) apart, in March/April: again in June/July, for use in autumn/following spring. Do not sow if the soil is cold and wet. Germination is often slow, taking 4-6 weeks. Assist by watering seed row with boiling water just before sowing. When 2nd set of leaves appears, thin seedlings to 15 cm. (6 ins.) apart. Summer raised plants can be covered with cloches, December onwards, to crop in early spring. Grow a few plants in pots in a greenhouse or on kitchen windowsill for winter use.

Parsnip
Hollow Crown

These Parsnips have long, smooth, tapering roots with tender flesh which has a slightly sweet taste. They produce a very large crop and can be harvested from October to March. Parsnips taste best after the first frost. May be grown for exhibition.

How to grow: Best in deep, fertile, well drained soil that is stone-free and of light or medium texture. Avoid freshly manured soil. Grow in a sunny position or one with light, partial shade.
Set 3-4 seeds, 1-2 cm. ($\frac{1}{2}$-$\frac{3}{4}$ in.) deep, and 15 cm. (6 ins.) apart with 30 cm. (1 ft.) between rows. For smaller roots, sow 8 cm. (3 ins.) apart with 20 cm. (8 ins.) between rows. In either case, when the 2nd set of leaves appears, thin the seedlings to leave one at each position. Sow from late February to May but not when the soil temperature is below 7°C. Water the crop well during dry weather. Lift the roots for use, as required, from October to March. Harvest any remaining parsnips in March, to prevent re-sprouting, and store in damp sand.

Radish
French Breakfast

Cylindrical radishes of bright scarlet, the lower portion being white in colour. They are very crisp and firm with a mild flavour. With their contrast of red and white, they look as good as they taste. Harvest May to October from outdoor sowings.

How to grow: Best in fairly rich, moist but well drained soil in a sunny position. Summer sowings can be made in light, partial shade. Avoid freshly manured soil.
Set seeds thinly, 2-2½ cm. (¾-1 in.) deep, in rows 10-15 cm. (4-6 ins.) apart. When the 2nd set of leaves appears, thin the seedlings to 2½ cm. (1 in.) apart. Sow some seeds every two weeks from March to September. By using cloches or a cold frame, sowings can be made in late February/early March and during September. Water well in dry weather. Harvest radishes when they are about 2 cm. (¾ in.) in diameter and still firm and crunchy.

Radish
Scarlet Globe

These are round, rich red radishes with fine, white flesh. They are firm and crisp, and have a mild flavour. Harvest May to October from outdoor sowings.

How to grow: Best in fairly rich, moist but well drained soil in a sunny position. Summer sowings can be made in light, partial shade. Avoid freshly manured soil.
Set seeds thinly, 2-2½ cm. (¾-1 in.) deep, in rows 10-15 cm. (4-6 ins.) apart. When the 2nd set of leaves appears, thin the seedlings to 2½ cm. (1 in.) apart. Sow some seeds every two weeks from March to September. By using cloches or a cold frame, sowings can be made in late February/early March and during September. Water well in dry weather. Harvest radishes when they are about 2 cm. (¾ in.) in diameter and still firm and crunchy. Scarlet Globe radishes can be cut so that they open out into rosettes when you put them in iced water.

Sage

A shrubby herb, 45-60 cm. (1½-2 ft.) tall, with strongly flavoured grey-green leaves, and violet-blue flowers in June/July. Use leaves in soups, stews and sauces; with pork, liver, duck and goose; in stuffings and with fish. Grow in the garden or in pots/window boxes.

How to grow: Best in well drained, fairly fertile soil with a little lime, in a sunny position. Hardy and lives for years. Raise new plants every 3-4 years for best results.

Under glass: Sow thinly, March/June, at 16-18°C in a greenhouse/indoors. When the 2nd set of leaves appears, transfer seedlings, 1 to an 8 cm. (3 ins.) pot. Grow on and, when the pots are well filled with roots, either harden off before planting out 40 cm. (15 ins.) apart, or transfer to 12 cm. (5 ins.) pots for window sill culture.

Outdoors: Sow thinly, 1 cm. (½ in.) deep, in prepared soil, April/June. Thin or transplant the young seedlings to 40 cm. (15 ins.) apart each way. Allow to become well established before cropping for the 1st time. Harvest top third of a few shoots from a plant at any one time. May also be cut for drying. Lightly cut back established plants in July, after flowering, to keep them bushy.

Spinach
Matador

Produces a succulent crop of large, smooth, dark green leaves which are ready to pick from May to October. Spinach is very nutritious and a welcome change of taste — use cooked, or the young leaves raw in salads. This variety is slow to run to seed.

How to grow: Likes a rich, well drained, but moisture-retentive soil, with a little lime. For best results add plenty of rotted manure/garden compost. Spinach tolerates light shade.

Set seeds thinly, 1-2 cm. (½-¾ in.) deep, in rows 30 cm. (1 ft.) apart. When the 2nd set of leaves appears, thin the seedlings to 8 cm. (3 ins.) apart. As the plants begin to touch each other, thin to 16 cm. (6 ins.) apart — these thinnings may be eaten. Sow some seeds every 2-3 weeks, March-July. By using cloches, a sowing can be made in late February provided the soil has warmed up. Keep the plants well watered in dry weather. Harvest regularly. Take some of the outside leaves on each occasion, picking them as near to the ground as possible. Alternatively, cut a whole plant about 3 cm. (1 in.) above soil level and leave it to re-sprout.

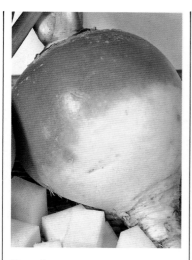

Swede
Magnificent

These swedes are large and very hardy with firm, yellow flesh which is milder and sweeter than that of turnips. Harvest from September right through to March. Large swedes can be hollowed out, faces cut in them and candles put inside for Hallowe'en parties.

How to grow: Best in fertile, well drained but moisture-retentive soil, with a little lime, in an open position. Avoid freshly manured soil.
Sow thinly, 2-2½ cm. (¾-1 in.) deep, in rows 40 cm. (15 ins.) apart, in early May (north), or during late May/early June (south). When the 2nd set of leaves appears, thin the seedlings to 22 cm. (9 ins.) apart. Keep the plants watered during dry weather to improve root size and quality. Harvest, as required for use, from September onwards. Though hardy, the roots can be lifted towards the end of December — to prevent possible coarseness or woodiness — and stored in boxes of damp sand in a cool, frost-free place.

Thyme

An aromatic herb, 22-30 cm. (9-12 ins.) tall, with narrow, dark green leaves and, from June, small, mauve flowers. Grow in the garden, in window boxes or in pots on a window sill. Use the leaves with meat, fish and vegetables, in soups, stews and sauces, or raw in salads.

How to grow: Best in well drained, fairly fertile soil with a little lime, in a sunny position. Hardy and lives for years. Raise new plants every 3 years, for best results.

Under glass: Sow thinly, March/June, at 13°C in a greenhouse/indoors. When the 2nd set of leaves appears, transfer seedlings, 1 to an 8 cm. (3 ins.) pot. Grow on and, when the pots are well filled with roots, either harden off before planting out 30 cm. (1 ft.) apart, or transfer to 11-12 cm. (4½-5 ins.) pots for window sill culture.

Outdoors: Sow thinly, ½ cm. (¼ in.) deep, in prepared soil, mid March/June. Thin or transplant the young seedlings to 30 cm. (1 ft.) apart each way. Allow to become well established before cropping for the first time. Harvest top third of a few stems from a plant at any one time. May also be cut for drying.

Tomato
The Amateur

An easy-to-grow bush variety, for outdoor cultivation, which reaches about 40 cm. (15 ins.) in height. Each plant produces up to 1.8 kg. (4 lbs.) of medium sized tomatoes from the end of July/early August to October.

How to grow: Best in fertile, well drained moisture-retentive soil in a sheltered, sunny position. Avoid over-rich conditions which encourage excessive foliage.

Sow thinly, 2 cm. (¾ in.) deep, in April at 18°C, in a greenhouse/indoors. When 2nd set of leaves appears, transfer seedlings, 1 to and 8 cm. (3 ins.) pot. Grow on in warmth and good light, then harden off — for example, in a cold frame — before planting out in early June (under cloches, latter half of May, if soil warmed up beforehand) at 48 cm. (19 ins.) apart each way. Plants may also be set in grow-bags. Do not 'stop' the plants or remove side shoots, nor is staking necessary. As fruit develops, place straw beneath the plants to keep the fruits clean. Pick tomatoes once they are ripe. Harvest all fruit before frost damage; ripen off indoors in a warm place, or use for chutney.

Tomato Gardener's Delight

Produces luscious, 'bite-sized' fruits that are rich, sweet and of delicious flavour. The plants carry a heavy crop of fruit on long trusses. For outdoors or greenhouse, grown on a single stem or as a bush.

Outdoor cropping: Sow thinly, 2 cm. (¾ in.) deep, late March/April, at 18°C in a greenhouse/indoors. Transfer seedlings, 1 to 8 cm. (3 ins.) pot. Grow in warmth and good light, then harden off before planting out, early June, at 40 cm. (15 ins.) apart each way when grown on a single stem; 48 cm. (19 ins.) apart as a bush. For single stem, support each plant with a 1.2 m. (4 ft.) cane, remove side shoots as they appear and pinch out growing point when 4 trusses have set. As bushes, do not 'stop' the plants or remove side shoots. A short stake is beneficial.

Greenhouse cropping: Sow as above, March/early April, and plant into 8 cm. (3 ins.) pots. Maintain minimum of 16°C at young plant stage. Grow as a single stem. Set out, when 15-22 cm. (6-9 ins.) tall, in growing bags or 45 cm. (18 ins.) apart each way in the border. Can be grown by Ring Culture or 1 plant to a 22 cm. (9 ins.) pot. Provide support for the plants. Start feeding with tomato fertiliser once the first truss has set.

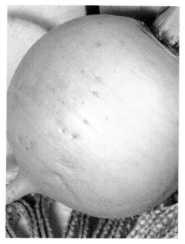

Tomato Moneymaker

Produces a heavy crop of medium sized tomatoes. This popular variety can be grown outdoors or in a greenhouse. Harvest June to October from greenhouse grown plants.

How to grow: Sow thinly, 2 cm. (¾ in.) deep, at 18°C in a greenhouse/indoors. Transfer young seedlings, 1 to an 8 cm. (3 ins.) pot. Grow in good light and warmth, with minimum of 16°C at young plant stage. Sow Jan./Feb. for heated greenhouse cultivation; otherwise March/April. Plant out, when 15-22 cm. (6-9 ins.) tall, 45 cm. (18 ins.) apart each way in a prepared greenhouse border; or use growing bags. May also be grown 1 plant to a 22 cm. (9 ins.) pot or, by Ring Culture, using 22 cm. (9 ins.) bottomless pots stood on 15 cm. (6 ins.) layer of pebbles/ashes. Remove side shoots, provide support for the plants and 'stop' them at the 6-7 truss stage. Start feeding with tomato fertiliser once the first truss has set. For outdoors, harden off before planting out in early June, 40 cm. (15 ins.) apart each way, in a sunny, sheltered position. Provide support, remove all side shoots and 'stop' the plants when 4 trusses have set.

Turnip
Golden Ball

A hardy, globe-shaped variety with rich yellow flesh which is juicy with a slightly sweet taste. Good for winter storage, and the tops may be grown to produce 'spring greens'.

How to grow: Best in fertile, moisture-retentive soil, with a little lime. Avoid freshly manured soil. Choose an open position or, for summer sowings, one in light, partial shade. Sow very thinly, 2-2½ cm. (¾-1 in.) deep, in rows 30 cm. (1 ft.) apart. When the 2nd set of leaves appears, thin seedlings to 8 cm. (3 ins.) apart and later, before plants start to touch, to 16 cm. (6 ins.). Sow July/early August to harvest in November for winter use. Store the roots in damp sand in a cool, frost-free place. In mild areas, lift turnips from the ground, as required. Make sowings at 3-4 week intervals, April/July, for young turnips, June/October. Plants should be 10 cm. (4 ins.) apart with 22 cm. (9 ins.) between rows. For 'spring greens', sow thinly, late August/Sept., in rows 16 cm. (6 ins.) apart. Do not thin. Cut — down to 3 cm. (1 in.) above the soil — March/April, when leaves are 10-16 cm. (4-6 ins.) tall. Re-sprouting will occur so that further croppings can be made.

Turnip
Purple Top Milan

A tasty, early variety with flat-shaped roots that are white with a reddish purple top. Harvest late May to October from successional sowings.

How to grow: Best in fertile, well drained but moisture-retentive soil, with a little lime. Avoid freshly manured soil. Choose an open position or, for summer sowings, one in light, partial shade.

Set the seeds very thinly, 2-2½ cm. (¾-1 in.) deep, in rows 22 cm. (9 ins.) apart. When the 2nd set of leaves appears, thin seedlings to 10 cm. (4 ins.) apart. Make a first sowing under cloches (which are removed later) in March to have turnips in late May or early June. Successional sowings, without cloche protection, should be made at 3-4 week intervals from April to July. Keep the plants well watered during dry weather. Harvest the roots while they are still young and tasty. They make a fine cooked vegetable or may be grated raw in salads.

Peas

Peas grow best in deeply cultivated, fertile soil that is well-drained but moisture-retentive. Dig in a 2 ins. layer of rotted manure or garden compost, preferably in winter before sowing. Choose an open but not exposed position. All peas will need to be supported. Provide support when tendrils appear, using netting, wire mesh, twiggy sticks or canes and twine. Place supports on either side of the bands. Water during dry spells when plants are flowering and producing pods. Harvest regularly when pods are young and fresh to encourage more to develop. When crop is over cut off stems at ground level and compost them. But leave the roots to release their nitrogen into the soil.

Pea Meteor

Early, round-seeded with a fine crop of pointed pods up to 3 ins. long from late May to late June onwards. Recommended for early sowings. Height 15 ins.

Pea Feltham First

Early, round-seeded with a good crop of pointed pods up to 3½ ins. long from late May to late June onwards. Recommended for early sowings. Height 18 ins.

For both varieties, sow during February (under cloches) or in early March (where sheltered, and if the soil is not cold and wet) for crops early/late June. To harvest late May/June, sow the previous October/November outdoors in mild areas, but give cloche protection, elsewhere, until March. Successional sowings can also be made March/July but wrinkled-seeded varieties are particularly recommended for this purpose. Set seeds about 5 cm. (2 ins.) apart in single rows, in a V-shaped drill 3-4 cm. (1-1½ ins.) deep, with 40 cm. (15 ins.) between rows. Alternatively, sow in 3-row bands. each row being 11 cm. (4½ ins.) apart. with seeds 11 cm. (4½ ins.) apart in the rows. Allow 45 cm. (18 ins.) between bands. To prevent birds digging up the seeds or eating the young seedlings. put hoop-shaped. fine-meshed wire netting over the rows. Set traps or put down bait to control mice.

Pea Onward

High-yielding. wrinkle-seeded and of a very good flavour and quality. Blunt-ended pods 4 ins. long growing in pairs from July to September. with successional sowings. Takes about 13–14 weeks from sowing to the first cropping. Suitable for freezing. Height 2½ ft.

Pea Hurst Green Shaft

Heavy-cropping. sweet-flavoured. with curved. pointed pods about 4½ ins. long. borne in pairs from late June/early July to September with successional sowings. Takes 12–13 weeks from sowing to first cropping. Suitable for freezing. Height 27–30 ins.

Pea Kelvedon Wonder

Early. very heavy cropping. wrinkle-seeded and of fine flavour with an abundance of well filled. dark-green pointed pods up to 3½ ins. long from late June to early October. with successional sowings. Takes 11–12 weeks from sowing to the first cropping. Suitable for freezing. Height 18–20 ins.

Snap Pea Sugar Rae

Snap Peas produce a heavy crop of thick. fleshy pods about 3 ins. long which are delicious to eat. Pick the young pods when they are round and full: trim and cook them whole. If preferred. Snap Peas can be shelled. the peas and pods being served separately. Also delicious. when young. chopped raw in salads. Harvest late June/early July to September with successional sowings. Height 2 ft.

For all these varieties make successional sowings. in prepared ground. every 3–4 weeks from late March to early July for harvesting late June to early October. Cloche protection may be required in October if early frosts occur.

Set seeds about 5 cm. (2 ins.) apart in single rows. in a V-shaped drill 3-4 cm. (1-1½ ins.) deep. with 45 cm. (18 ins.) between rows. Alternatively, sow in 3-row bands. each row being 11 cm. (4½ ins.) apart. with seeds 11 cm. (4½ ins.) apart in the rows. Allow 45 cm. (18 ins.) between bands. To prevent birds digging up the seeds or eating the young seedlings. put hoop-shaped. fine-meshed wire netting over the rows. Set traps or put down bait to control mice.

Beans

How to grow: Beans grow best in deeply-cultivated, fertile soil which is well-drained but is moisture retentive. Sow in a warm, sheltered spot. Broad beans and Dwarf French beans need a 2" layer of rotted manure or garden compost dug into the soil the winter before sowing. Runner beans need a 27" wide trench dug to a spade's depth in the winter or early spring before sowing. Fill the bottom with well rotted manure or garden compost and replace the soil. Then 1–2 weeks before sowing hoe in a general fertiliser.

Runner beans. Sow mid to late May (as long as soil temp. is 10-12°C) to harvest for early August. Set seed 1–1½" deep and 6" apart in double rows with 2 ft. between each row. If more than one double row then allow 3 ft. between each. Sow a few seeds at the end of each row to replace any that don't come up.

For earlier crops sow under cloches mid/late April putting them in position 3–4 weeks before sowing. Leave cloches over the plants until mid June. Can sow individually in small pots in a cool greenhouse about 4 weeks before planting out time which should be after the last frost. For support use 2.4 m. (8 ft.) canes — 1 to a plant — and put them in position before sowing or when plants are 8-10 cm. (3-4 ins.) tall. Cross over the canes in pairs and tie them at the top.

Tie a horizontal cane along the top of the row for stability. Support may also be given using bean netting, or a tripod or wigwam of canes. Water in dry weather during the flowering and cropping period. Pick regularly, when the beans are young and tender, to encourage more to develop. Pinch out growing points when plants reach the top of the supports. When the crop is over, cut off the stems at ground level and compost them, but leave the roots in the soil to release their nitrogen.

Dwarf French beans. To harvest late May until September, sow January/February under cloches (leaving them in position until late March/early April), and in prepared, open ground, at 2-3 week intervals, from March to May. A sowing can be made in a warm sheltered position outdoors during late October/November to harvest late May/early June to July.

Set seeds 4-5 cm. (1½-2 ins.) deep and 11 cm. (4½ ins.) apart with 45 cm. (18 ins.) between rows. Sow a few extra of the seeds at the end of the row to replace any that do not come up. Support the plants with canes or stakes (with 90-120 cm./3-4 ft. of their length above soil level) and twine, the strands of twine being attached at 30 cm. (1 ft.) intervals as growth develops. When in full flower, pinch out the main growing tips of each plant to discourage black fly attack and to assist pod development. Water during dry spells when the plants are flowering and producing pods. Harvest regularly, when the pods are young and fresh, to encourage more to develop. When the crop is over, cut off the stems at ground level and compost them, but leave the roots to release their nitrogen into the soil.

Broad beans. For harvesting from late June/early July, sow under cloches in early April, putting them in position 3-4 weeks before sowing and leaving them over the plants until June. Make outdoor sowings (provided the soil temperature is at least 10-12°C), at monthly intervals, from late April (in south) or early May (north) until July. A sowing in mid July will provide crops during the mid September/October period, but cover the plants with cloches in September to protect them from frost. Set the seeds in prepared ground, 4-5 cm. (1½-2 ins.) deep and 5-8 cm. (2-3 ins.) apart with 45 cm. (18 ins.) between rows. To achieve maximum yields, do not thin out the plants. Staking is not necessary but the plants can be supported with twiggy sticks to keep the lower leaves off the

ground and the pods clean. When the plants are in flower, keep the plants well watered during dry weather. Harvest regularly, when the pods are 12-15 cm. (5-6 ins.) long and still young and tender, to encourage more to develop. Dwarf French Beans produce plenty of leaves, so look under them to see if the pods are ready. When the crop is over, cut off the stems at ground level and compost them, but leave the roots to release their nitrogen into the soil.

SOWING INDEX

JANUARY

Sow
Geranium (glass)
Broad Bean (glass)
Cauliflower (glass)
Onion (glass)
Tomato (heated greenhouse)

FEBRUARY

Sow
Alyssum (glass)
Antirrhinum (glass)
Carnation (glass)
Dahlia (glass)
Impatiens (glass)
Lobelia (glass)
Lupin (glass)
African Marigold (glass)
Mesembryanthemum (glass)
Nicotiana (glass)
Pansy (glass)
Petunia (glass)
Rudbeckia (glass)
Salvia (glass)
Statice (glass)
Sweet Pea (glass)
Tagetes (glass)
Broad bean (glass)
Beetroot (glass)
Cabbage (glass)
Cucumber (glass)
Onion (glass)
Parsley (glass)
Parsnip
Tomato (heated greenhouse)

MARCH

Sow
Ageratum
Alyssum (glass)
Antirrhinum (glass)
Aquilegia (glass)
Aster (glass)
Aubretia (glass)
Calendula
Canary Creeper (glass)
Candy tuft

Carnation
Clarkia
Cornflower
Dahlia (glass)
Helichrysum (glass)
Impatiens
Lobelia (glass)
Lupin (glass)
African Marigold (glass)
French Marigold (glass)
Mesembryanthemum (glass)
Morning Glory (glass)
Nicotiana (glass)
Pansy
Petunia (glass)
Polyanthus (glass)
Californian Poppy (glass)
Rudbeckia (glass)
Salvia (glass)
Stocks
Sunflower
Sweet Pea (glass)
Tagetes (glass)
Zinnia (glass)
Beetroot (cloche)
Broad bean
Brussels sprouts
Cabbage (glass)
Cauliflower (glass)
Celery
Chives
Cucumber (glass)
Leek
Lettuce
Onion
Parsley (glass)
Parsnip
Pea
Pea (snap)
Radish
Sage (glass)
Spinach
Thyme
Tomato

APRIL

Sow
Ageratum
Alyssum
Antirrhinum
Aquilegia (glass)

Aster
Aubretia (glass)
Calendula
Canary Creeper
Candy tuft
Carnation (glass)
Clarkia
Cornflower
Dahlia (glass)
Godetia
Helichrysum
Lupin
African Marigold (glass)
French Marigold (glass)
Morning Glory (glass)
Nasturtium
Nicotiana (glass)
Pansy
Petunia (glass)
Polyanthus (glass)
Californian Poppy
Schizanthus (glass)
Stocks
Sunflower
Sweet Pea
Tagetes
Zinnia (glass)

Beet (leaf)
Beetroot
Broad bean
Broccoli (sprouting)
Brussels Sprouts
Cabbage
Carrots
Cauliflower
Celery
Chives
Cucumber (glass)
Dwarf French bean
Leek
Lettuce
Marrow (glass)
Onion
Parsley
Parsnip
Pea
Pea (snap)
Radish
Sage (glass)
Spinach
Thyme
Tomato
Turnip

MAY

Sow
Alyssum
Antirrhinum
Aquilegia
Aster
Aubretia
Calendula
Candy tuft
Canterbury Bells
Clarkia
Cornflower
Double Daisy
Delphinium
Forget Me Not
Godetia
Helichrysum
Lupin
French Marigold
Nasturtium
Nemesia
Polyanthus (glass)
Californian Poppy
Stocks
Sunflower
Sweet Pea
Sweet William
Tagetes
Wallflower
Zinnia

Beet (leaf)
Beetroot
Broad bean
Broccoli (sprouting)
Cabbage
Carrots
Cauliflower
Chives
Cucumber (glass)
Dwarf French bean
Lettuce
Marrow/Zucchini
Pea
Pea (snap)
Radish
Runner bean
Sage
Spinach
Swede
Thyme
Turnip

JUNE

Sow
Aquilegia
Aubretia (glass)
Calendula
Candy tuft
Canterbury Bells
Cornflower
Double Daisy
Delphinium
Forget Me Not
Godetia
Lupin
French Marigold
Nemesia
Polyanthus (glass)
Californian Poppy
Brompton Stock
Stocks
Sweet William
Wallflower
Beetroot
Carrots
Chives
Cucumber
Dwarf French Bean
Lettuce
Marrow/Zucchini
Parsley
Pea
Radish
Sage
Spinach
Swede
Thyme
Turnip

JULY

Sow
Aquilegia
Aubretia (glass)
Lupin
Brompton Stock
Beet (leaf)
Beetroot
Carrots
Dwarf French bean
Lettuce
Parsley
Pea
Radish
Spinach
Turnip

AUGUST

Sow
Lettuce
Radish
Turnip
Autumn onions (seedbed)
Spring Cabbage
Winter Spinach

SEPTEMBER

Sow
Lettuce
Radish
Salad onions
Winter Spinach

OCTOBER

Sow
Cauliflower (glass)
Cabbage (seedbed)

NOVEMBER

Sow
Broad beans (hardy)
Peas (early)

DECEMBER

Sow
Broad beans (hardy)

HARVEST/BLOOM INDEX

JANUARY

Harvest/Bloom
Brussels sprouts
Leek
Parsnip
Swede

FEBRUARY

Harvest/Bloom
Broccoli (sprouting)
Brussels sprouts
Cauliflower
Leek
Parsnip
Swede

MARCH

Harvest/Bloom
Aubretia
Polyanthus
Broccoli (sprouting)
Cauliflower
Leek
Swede

APRIL

Harvest/Bloom
Aubretia
Double Daisy
Forget Me Not
Polyanthus
Wallflower
Sprouting broccoli
Red Cabbage
Spring Cabbage
Spring onions

MAY

Harvest/Bloom
Aquilegia
Aubretia
Double Daisy
Forget Me Not
Lupin
Pansy
Polyanthus
Brompton Stock
Wallflower
Beet (leaf)

Broad bean
Cabbage
Chives
Cucumber
Lettuce
Radish
Spinach

JUNE

Harvest/Bloom
Ageratum
Alyssum
Antirrhinum
Aquilegia
Aubretia
Calendula
Candy tuft
Canterbury Bells
Cornflower
Double Daisy
Delphinium
Forget Me Not
Godetia
Impatiens
Lobelia
Lupin
African Marigold
French Marigold
Mesembryanthemum
Nasturtium
Nemesia
Nicotiana
Pansy
Petunia
Californian Poppy
Schizanthus
Brompton Stock
Sweet Pea
Sweet William
Wallflower
Beet
Broad bean
Cabbage
Cauliflower
Chives
Cucumber
Dwarf French Bean
Lettuce
Parsley
Pea
Radish
Sage

Spinach
Thyme
Tomato

JULY

Harvest/Bloom

Ageratum
Alyssum
Antirrhinum
Aster
Calendula
Canary Creeper
Candy tuft
Canterbury Bells
African Marigold
French Marigold
Mesembryanthemum
Morning Glory
Nasturtium
Nemesia
Nicotiana
Pansy
Petunia
Californian Poppy
Rudbeckia
Salvia
Schizanthus
Statice
Stocks
Sunflower
Sweet Pea
Sweet William
Tagetes
Zinnia
Beet (leaf)
Beetroot
Broad bean
Cabbage
Cauliflower
Chives
Cucumber
Dwarf French Beans
Lettuce
Marrow/Zucchini
Parsley
Pea
Pea (snap)
Radish
Runner Bean
Sage
Spinach
Thyme
Tomato
Turnip

AUGUST

Harvest/Bloom

Ageratum
Alyssum
Antirrhinum
Aster
Calendula
Canary Creeper
Candy tuft
Carnation
Clarkia
Cornflower
Dahlia
Delphinium
Geranium
Godetia
Helichrysum
Impatiens
Lobelia
African Marigold
French Marigold
Mesembryanthemum
Morning Glory
Nasturtium
Nemesia
Nicotiana
Pansy
Petunia
Californian Poppy
Rudbeckia
Salvia
Schizanthus
Statice
Stocks
Sunflower
Sweet Pea
Tagetes
Zinnia
Beet (leaf)
Beetroot
Broad Bean
Cabbage
Carrots
Cauliflower
Celery
Chives
Cucumber
Lettuce
Marrow/Zucchini
Onion
Parsley
Pea
Pea (snap)
Radish
Runner Bean

Sage
Spinach
Thyme
Tomato
Turnip

SEPTEMBER

Harvest/Bloom
Ageratum
Alyssum
Antirrhinum
Aster
Calendula
Canary Creeper
Candy tuft
Carnation
Clarkia
Cornflower
Dahlia
Geranium
Godetia
Helichrysum
Impatiens
Lobelia
African Marigold
French Marigold
Mesembryanthemum
Morning Glory
Nasturtium
Nemesia
Nicotiana
Pansy
Petunia
Californian Poppy
Rudbeckia
Salvia
Schizanthus
Statice
Stocks
Sunflower
Sweet Pea
Tagetes
Zinnia
Beet (leaf)
Beetroot
Broad Bean
Cabbage
Carrots
Celery
Chives
Dwarf French Bean
Lettuce
Marrow/Zucchini
Onion
Parsley

Pea
Pea (snap)
Radish
Runner Bean
Spinach
Swede
Tomato
Turnip

OCTOBER

Harvest/Bloom
Antirrhinum
Aster
Canary Creeper
Geranium
Impatiens
Lobelia
African Marigold
French Marigold
Californian Poppy
Rudbeckia
Schizanthus
Zinnia
Beet (leaf)
Carrots
Leek
Parsley
Parsnip
Pea
Radish
Runner Bean
Spinach
Swede
Tomato
Turnip
Winter Spinach

NOVEMBER

Harvest/Bloom
Beetroot (maincrop)
Brussels sprouts
Leek
Parsnip
Swede
Turnip
Winter Spinach

DECEMBER

Harvest/Bloom
Brussels sprouts
Leek
Parsnip
Swede
Winter Spinach
Turnips

YOUR WEEKLY RECORD

JANUARY

_____

_____

_____

_____

_____

_____

_____

_____

FEBRUARY

_____

_____

_____

_____

_____

_____

_____

_____

MARCH

_____
_____
_____
_____
_____
_____
_____

APRIL

_____
_____
_____
_____
_____
_____
_____

MAY

_____

_____

_____

_____

_____

_____

_____

_____

JUNE

_____

_____

_____

_____

_____

_____

_____

_____

JULY

_____
_____
_____
_____
_____
_____
_____

AUGUST

_____
_____
_____
_____
_____
_____
_____

SEPTEMBER

OCTOBER

NOVEMBER

_____

_____

_____

_____

_____

_____

_____

DECEMBER

_____

_____

_____

_____

_____

_____

_____

NOTES

_____

_____

_____

_____

_____

_____

_____

_____

_____

_____

_____

_____

_____

_____

_____

_____

_____

_____

NOTES

NOTES

Production: Mercurius U.K.
Layout: T. J. Wright, D. Lester
Pictures: Carters Tested Seeds Ltd and Harry Smith Horticultural Photographic
Collection
Printing: BV Kunstdrukkerij Mercurius-Wormerveer
Typesetting: S M Studios, Colchester
Author: Tony Loynes

This edition published by Sphere Books Ltd., London 1984 in association with
Carters Tested Seeds Ltd. The publishers are grateful to Carters Tested Seeds
Ltd for supplying the pictures and text from their seed packets for the alphabetical
glossary.